NAKED

The Lyrics and the Lifeline

Table of Contents

Introduction: The Context and The Confession

The title of this book, **Naked**, is not a suggestion—it's an **uncompromising mandate**. It is a promise to the reader that I will open my innermost feelings to the world without a filter, and a challenge to myself not to hold anything back, no matter how painful or intensely vulnerable the truth may be. The lyrics of a song often tell a story and a collection of songs from the same lyricist can position those within a wider story, which is the case for the lyrics shared here.

For years, I've listened to friends tell me I am too open, too emotional, too quick to expose my inner landscape. But as a team coach and someone deeply engaged in reflective psychology, I've come to believe the opposite: that the greatest source of human stress and suffering is the fear of our own emotions. We are constantly trained to wear **armour**, to suppress the ugly, the painful, or the deeply vulnerable truth. It is the unrelenting effort of keeping that armour polished and sealed—the **"invisible checklist"** of performance and perfection—that ultimately breaks us down and separates us from authentic connection. This book is my counter-argument. It is my exploration of what happens when you decide to **strip that armour away** and accept your flaws as your greatest source of power.

My typical approach to writing starts not with a plan, but with a **powerful burst of inspiration** or a significant emotional burden. The act of turning to the page is a necessity—it helps me to articulate and clarify the precise, messy emotion I need to process. This initial, raw reflection generates the central, undeniable idea, or **seed,** for the song's chorus. Once that initial, resonant core is established, I compile a list of related personal experiences, observations, or synthesised emotions. This list serves as the pool of concrete imagery and concepts from which I pull ideas for the narrative and metaphor of the verses, transforming chaotic feelings into a structured story. This initial act of self-articulation began as poetry for processing raw experiences, and that reflective practice evolved into songwriting, which offered a necessary structure for taking overwhelming emotion and **refining it into something universal and articulate.**

This is not a traditional memoir or a simple book of poetry. This book is a detailed look behind the curtain of the creative process. Instead of chapters, you will find song entries, and each one is structured to tell **three concurrent stories**:

- **The Story of the Soul (The Why):** The intense feeling or personal paradox that served as the emotional seed for the song's Chorus.
- **The Story of the Craft (The How):** My process of translating that raw emotion and the synthesised experiences of others into the structured narrative, metaphor, and profound ideas that make up the Verses.
- **The Lifeline (The Listen):** A direct link to the **SoundCloud demo** for the track, providing the musical context and emotional rhythm that gave life to my final lyric. The essence of lyrics is that they are open to interpretation by a performer. The samples you can hear are representative of what I heard in my head while writing the lyrics.

My goal in sharing these "Naked" lyrics and their origins is to give you permission to feel the entire range of your own experience. Because only when we stop fearing our own vulnerability can we truly begin to live, to connect, and to create. We stop running from who we were, and start celebrating the messy, winding path that made us who we are now.

The songs are not presented in chronological order but are listed in Parts of related sentiment or meaning. You can jump straight to lyrics that might interest you although that is not my main aim for this book. I hope that I am able to provide an insight into my process in approaching the task of translating an idea into a lyric (or indeed a poem).

Contents

Part I: The Descent and the Reckoning (Songs 1-9)

The exploration of internal conflict, relationship crisis, and the initial surrender to pain.

Part II: The Rebuilding and the Anchors (Songs 10-17)

The slow, deliberate work of healing, establishing boundaries, reconnecting with self-worth, and finding healthy support.

Part III: The Transcendence and The Human Power (Songs 18-22)

The final resolution, where growth is cemented, and the narrator embraces a resilient, imperfect identity.

Part I: The Descent and the Reckoning (Songs 1-9)

The exploration of internal conflict, relationship crisis, and the initial surrender to pain.

1. Letting Go

The Story of the Soul (The Why)

Inspiration: Conversations with military veterans and suicide attempt survivors, including my son, revealing that the endpoint is often not sharp pain or desperation, but numbness, resignation, and a lack of fight.

What I Was Trying to Portray: I wanted to create a song that corrects the common misconception of suicide, showing that it can be a slow, quiet surrender rather than a dramatic, painful crisis. I intended to portray the experience of the person who has reached total, emotional depletion, where they are merely acting out a role for the outside world while the self has already checked out.

The Intentional Feeling: I was aiming to express a feeling of profound, hopeless emptiness and a weary resignation. The goal was to articulate the seductive "sweet, quiet comfort of severing chains"—the relief of simply stopping the exhausting performance of life.

The Story of the Craft (The How)

How I Chose to Portray It: I deliberately used metaphors that emphasised absence and performance to show the protagonist's emotional state. The structure moves from the protagonist's external mask, through their internal emptiness, to the final moment of quiet surrender.

The Chosen Focus: I focused on contrasting the exterior world with the interior reality:

The External Mask: Using imagery like "nod and I smile," "Play the part," and a "monotone grace" to show the effort required to maintain a façade for others.

The Internal Emptiness: Using metaphors of "hollowed-out echo" and "cement in its chest" to describe the feeling of numbness that replaces emotional pain, directly reflecting the quiet desperation your friends described.

The Final Surrender (Bridge): I made the climax about relief, not fear. Phrases like "tension finally leaving my bones" and "let go of the crown" were chosen to portray the desired state of floating down rather than drowning—the ultimate cessation of effort.

The Lifeline (The Listen):
https://on.soundcloud.com/oROQSvEIUWkFd2XSrw

The Lyrics

[Verse 1]

I still stand in line, I still nod and I smile

Play the part for a minute, just for a short while

I tie up my laces, I walk out the door

But the face that you see isn't mine anymore.

It's a hollowed-out echo, a ghost in the street

With cement in its chest instead of a heartbeat

I answer your questions with a monotone grace

And pray that the light doesn't shatter this place.

[Chorus]

The pain has faded; there's no more to see

It is just a hopeless emptiness I feel deep

I really have no fight left within me

I will gladly accept a permanent sleep

[Verse 2]

I look out the window at the people who dream

They cling to their faith, they ride the mainstream

But that current is shallow, and I've long let go

There's nothing to chase, there's nothing to know.

I see every flicker of light you still hold

And I envy the stories that you're waiting to be told.

It's a comfort to know that this shell isn't real

A weight I'm prepared to stop trying to heal.

[Chorus]

The pain has faded; there's no more to see

It is just a hopeless emptiness I feel deep

I really have no fight left within me

I will gladly accept a permanent sleep

[Verse 3]

I trace the blue lines running back on my hand,

A roadmap of failures I don't understand.

I reach for the bottle, a comfort I know,

But the weight of the gesture just makes me let go.

The glass hits the floor and the shatter is clean,

The last sound I'll make in this silent-film scene.

I just sink in the chair, and I stare at the pane,

Trying hard to remember the feeling of rain—

Not the storm and the sorrow, but the genuine joy

That the child in this body was built to enjoy.

[Bridge]

I can feel the tension finally leaving my bones

The pressure of keeping up, the heavy stones

And it isn't fear that runs cold through my veins

It's the sweet, quiet comfort of severing chains.

I just want to stop swimming, I just want to float down.

Take off the armor, let go of the crown.

[Chorus]

The pain has faded; there's no more to see

It is just a hopeless emptiness I feel deep

I really have no fight left within me

I will gladly accept a permanent sleep

[Outro]

No fight left...

Just the deep...

Just the deep, quiet...

(Music slowly fades to silence)

2. The Eulogy

The Story of the Soul (The Why)

Inspiration: This song was inspired by an old Irish funeral lament and my observation that the real eulogy happens at the wake—where people gather to share stories and memories—rather than in the formal church service.

What I Was Trying to Portray: My core intent was to give the departed a final, powerful voice, using that voice to command a celebration of life over grief. I wanted to portray death not as an end, but as a change in location ("I'm not gone, I'm just not here"), making the continuation of joy the highest form of tribute.

The Intentional Feeling: I aimed for a feeling of uplifting, communal defiance against sorrow. The mood is one of warmth, camaraderie, and deep gratitude, culminating in a final, peaceful instruction: "Miss me, love me, but let me go." This should feel like a loving release for those left behind.

The Story of the Craft (The How)

How I Chose to Portray It: I deliberately placed the song entirely in the first-person voice of the deceased speaking directly to the mourners. I used clear, action-oriented language to replace passive grief with active celebration ("raise a glass," "tell the stories," "dance through the night").

The Chosen Focus: I focused on two main areas to communicate the message:

The Rejection of Ritual Sorrow: I explicitly dismissed traditional symbols of mourning, telling the attendees to "see

17

through the grey" (the black clothing) and "Don't chase a ghost or hold a tear." The emphasis is that this ceremony is "for joy we hold dear," not sorrow.

The Presence in Memory: I established that the speaker remains present through sensory experience and communal actions—"laughter and warmth," being found "in the breezes that blow" and the "stars in the sky." The craft links the departed's "flame" to the continuation of shared memories, making every story told a reaffirmation of life.

The Lifeline (The Listen):

https://on.soundcloud.com/VbaIJBcpkrlzpuBvry

The Lyric

[Verse 1]

In the morning light when the world wakes slow,

You'll find the strength in the love that you know.

They're all in black, but I see through the grey,

Lift up your hearts, don't let them fade away.

We've danced through the years, spun gold from the sun,

So here's a toast to all the battles we've won.

With laughter and warmth, we've shared every tear,

This day ain't for sorrow; it's for joy we hold dear.

[Chorus]

So raise a glass, don't let it fall,

And tell the stories, friends, one and all.

In the shadows, let's find the light,

You know my flame still burns so bright.

Don't chase a ghost or hold a tear,

For I'm not gone, I'm just not here.

Remember the joy, the life we'd know,

Just "Miss me, love me, but let me go."

[Verse 2]

The laughter we shared on those sun-kissed days

Can still be found in life's funny ways.

Each story we wrote, every song we strung,

Plays in the echoes of the hearts we've won.

So gather 'round, let the memories flow,

Let's sing out the tunes from the times we'd glow.

For every smile, I'll be standing near,

In every sweet whisper, you'll know that I'm here.

[Chorus]

So raise a glass, don't let it fall,

And tell the stories, friends, one and all.

In the shadows, let's find the light,

You know my flame still burns so bright.

Don't chase a ghost or hold a tear,

For I'm not gone, I'm just not here.

Remember the joy, the life we'd know,

Just "Miss me, love me, but let me go."

[Bridge]

Dance through the night with the stars in the sky,

With every beat, lift your heart up high.

This ain't a day for bowed heads or sighs,

We'll celebrate life; let our spirits rise.

You'll find me in the breezes that blow,

In the warmth of the sun, that's where I'll show.

I'm there in your laughter, I'm found in your dreams,

So live out your days; let your heart burst at the seams.

[Final Chorus]

So raise a glass, don't let it fall,

And tell the stories, friends, one and all.

In the shadows, let's find the light,

You know my flame still burns so bright.

Don't chase a ghost or hold a tear,

For I'm not gone, I'm just not here.

Remember the joy, the life we'd know,

Just "Miss me, love me, but let me go."

[Outro]

So as the sun sets and the stars align,

Remember the laughter, the love, the time.

Lift up your spirits, let the memories flow,

"Miss me, love me, but let me go."

3. Deafening Silence

The Story of the Soul (The Why)

Inspiration: The lingering, unconscious habits of a life shared—setting out a second cup of tea, smelling phantom perfume, or instinctively avoiding ingredients she disliked while shopping. The hardest moment is the isolation of lying awake in bed.

What I Was Trying to Portray: I wanted to communicate that the pain of separation is less about a single dramatic loss and more about the hundreds of tiny, reflexive habits that survive the breakup. I intended to show how the mundane repetition of routine becomes a trigger for grief, highlighting the emotional exhaustion of constantly editing a life built for two.

The Intentional Feeling: I aimed to capture the paradox of "deafening silence," where the lack of her physical presence is replaced by the overwhelming, "loud" noise of memory and loneliness. This feeling is characterised by restlessness, physical discomfort ("toss and I turn"), and sleeplessness.

The Story of the Craft (The How)

How I Chose to Portray It: I used a narrative structure built around common household routines and everyday journeys to make the grief visceral and immediate. The verses function as a catalogue of unconscious, automated actions that are now forced to stop.

The Chosen Focus: I focused on specific sensory and action-based details to convey the slow, stubborn nature of change:

The Sensory Ghost (Verse 1): I opened with the attempted comfort of a familiar smell ("caught a scent in the air") that quickly becomes a painful truth, immediately establishing that absence is more powerful than the faint memory.

The Habitual Mistake (Verses 1 & 2): I used the concrete actions of setting out two cups for tea and picking up the red wine only to put it back. These details illustrate that the brain and body are still operating in "couple mode," and the cancellation of the action is the daily, painful reminder of loss.

The Echoing Landscape (Verse 3): I used external, shared geography ("Drove down the street where we used to roam," "The cafe we loved") to show that the world itself has become a container of memories, every place whispering "the tales of our home."

The Paradox in the Chorus: I tied the physical sleeplessness and tossing/turning to the central paradox of the "deafening silence," making the lack of sound the most intrusive sound of all.

The Lifeline (The Listen):

https://on.soundcloud.com/917hz2UbigF60ZJWc5

The Lyrics

[Verse 1]

I woke up this morning, the sun in the sky,

But something's different, I don't know why.

I walked through the house, caught a scent in the air,

But it's not your perfume—'cause you're not there.

I put out two cups to make us some tea,

It's just an old habit, but it still hurts me.

I guess small things take a little longer to change,

This whole damn house just feels so strange.

[Chorus]

'Cause the silence is deafening, keeping me awake,

Every tick of the clock is a sound I can't take.

I toss and I turn and I pull at the sheets,

But all that's around me is these lonely heartbeats.

And the memories, they're so loud in my mind,

A deafening silence is all I can find.

[Verse 2]

Went to the market, the usual time,

Walked by the aisle—your favourite red wine.

Picked up a bottle, like I've done before,

Then I put it back down and walked out the door.

'Cause what's the point in having a drink with a ghost?

I guess I'm just living on the echoes of us.

[Verse 3]

Drove down the street where we used to roam,

Every corner whispers the tales of our home.

I hear your laughter, it echoes in the air,

But the windows are empty, it's grief that I wear.

The café we loved has a table for two,

But honey, it's just me, and I'm missing you.

[Chorus]

'Cause the silence is deafening, keeping me awake,

Every tick of the clock is a sound I can't take.

I toss and I turn and I pull at the sheets,

But all that's around me is these lonely heartbeats.

And the memories, they're so loud in my mind,

A deafening silence is all I can find.

[Bridge]

Found your letter stuck in an old book,

Opened it slowly, brought back the look.

Letters of love that now feel like chains,

Words once so soothing now echo with pain.

Can't escape the past, it keeps calling me back,

Like shadows at dusk on a haunting track.

[Chorus]

'Cause the silence is deafening, keeping me awake,

Every tick of the clock is a sound I can't take.

I toss and I turn and I pull at the sheets,

But all that's around me is these lonely heartbeats.

And the memories, they're so loud in my mind,

A deafening silence is all I can find.

[Outro]

So I'll lay my head down beneath this dark sky,

Whisper your name in the stillness, oh why?

Just know I'll keep living in the echoes divine,

In this silence, my dear, I'll remember our time.

4. Silence in the Room

The Story of the Soul (The Why)

Inspiration: Waking up after drinking to find hurtful, contradictory messages sent to a loved one, followed by the terrifying realisation of not remembering the messages and deeply disagreeing with their cruel content. The primary terror was that this reflected a deeper, buried psychological fracture that had now wounded someone dearly loved.

What I Was Trying to Portray: I intended to portray a severe crisis of self-identity, where the protagonist is literally confronted with a "stranger in my body." The message is the profound shame and fear of knowing your own hands and voice have betrayed the person you love most, and the resulting paranoia that a destructive "other" lives inside you.

The Intentional Feeling: A haunting self-betrayal, betrayal by one's own voice and hands. The feeling is one of desperate moral accounting and a fierce commitment to fight that internal "poison" for the sake of the person he loves.

The Story of the Craft (The How)

How I Chose to Portray It: I structured the song around the physical evidence of the betrayal (the glowing phone screen) and used metaphors of possession and digital communication to separate the protagonist's conscious will from his destructive actions.

The Chosen Focus: I focused on specific imagery to communicate disconnection and horror:

Digital Disassociation (Verse 1 & Chorus): The "tiny screen" and "my hands were just the keyboard" distance the true self from the act. The chorus confession—"I've been a servant to a poison, a puppet to a rage"—externalises blame onto the alcohol-fuelled state while still owning the consequence.

The Fractured Self (Verse 2): Visual metaphors of a "fractured, ugly portrait" and "tapestry of darkness" convey the shock of seeing a monstrous reflection. This verse is the search for "the person I don't know" in order to contain and heal him.

The Vow of Reclamation (Bridge): The turning point—moving from horror to resolve. "Sealing the devil's mouth" becomes the moral imperative: regaining absolute sovereignty over his own voice and actions.

The Lifeline (The Listen):

https://on.soundcloud.com/NAw4JYv9rE65125bNM

The Lyric

[Verse 1]

The morning came too fast, a stumble from the night,

With silence in the room, everything feels tight.

The tiny screen was humming, a ghost whispering near,

Words that echo sadness, a haunting that I fear.

The words were mine, the numbers right, but feelings were all

wrong, A stranger in my body singing a different song.

[Chorus]

How could I say those things? How could I be that cruel?

My hands were just the keyboard, my voice a willing tool.

I've been a servant to a poison, a puppet to a rage,

A good man writing venom on a digital white page.

[Verse 2]

Each click a reflection, each letter a disguise,

Unraveling this madness, the stranger in my eyes.

A fractured, ugly portrait, ragged at the seams,

A tapestry of darkness woven through my dreams.

There's a person I don't know trapped in skin and bone,

Searching for redemption in a world so overgrown.

[Chorus]

How could I say those things? How could I be that cruel?

My hands were just the keyboard, my voice a willing tool.

I've been a servant to a poison, a puppet to a rage,

A good man writing venom on a digital white page.

[Bridge]

I see a hundred tiny mirrors reflecting back the lies,

The madness in the message, pain buried under sighs.

This digital existence can't be my legacy,

I'll walk this path of shadows, seek the light inside of me.

I need to find the voice that's mine and seal the devil's mouth,

To silence every wicked thought before the words get out.

[Verse 3]

There's a whisper in the silence calling out my name,

Reminding me of kindness, to break free from the shame.

Regaining trust in sunshine, unwinding from the dark,

I'll rise above the ashes, ignite a brand-new spark.

Let every touch be healing, let every word be true,

Emerging from the shadows to embrace a world renewed.

[Chorus]

How could I say those things? How could I be that cruel?

My hands were just the keyboard, my voice a willing tool.

I've been a servant to a poison, a puppet to a rage,

A good man writing venom on a digital white page.

[Outro]

So here's my silent promise, to find the strength to change,

To forge my heart in kindness, no matter how it's strange.

The morning came too fast, but I won't let it stay—

I'll rewrite all those stories, find the light within the grey.

5. Good Servant, Poor Master

The Story of the Soul (The Why)

Inspiration: The experiences detailed in "Silence in the Room" forced a brutal self-interrogation about whether to give up drinking entirely. It crystallised in the phrase: "three is too many, four is not enough." The core truth is that explanation is never an excuse—actions taken under the influence are still the direct consequence of the decision to drink too much.

What I Was Trying to Portray: I wanted to portray the complex, almost tender relationship one has with a coping mechanism, balanced against the iron demand for radical accountability. The substance is a genuine "Good Servant" that offers real, temporary comfort, yet becomes a tyrannical "Poor Master" the moment control slips.

The Intentional Feeling: Clear-eyed resignation giving way to moral conviction. The mood moves from the soft seduction of escape to the unflinching, necessary truth of self-mastery.

The Story of the Craft (The How)

How I Chose to Portray It: I built the entire song around the ancient idiom of the title ("Good Servant, Poor Master") as an extended metaphor, assigning warm, comforting language to the servant and cold, controlling imagery to the master.

The Chosen Focus: Contrasting the promise with the price:

The Servant's Allure (Verse 1): Soft, soothing language—
"gentle lullaby," "press the pause button," "comfort in the
quiet"—to show exactly why the choice feels loving and safe.

-**The Master's Control (Chorus):** The servant morphs into
"a shadow that grows," turning the drinker into "a puppet on
a string" and exacting a "debt" that strips away freedom and
dignity.

The Consequence (Verse 2): Sensory deficit—"fog in my
head," "blurry line," "another broken promise"—directly
linking the drinking to the wounds inflicted in "Silence in the
Room."

The Lifeline (The Listen):
https://on.soundcloud.com/NRKuClf5YWGOShk6Uu

The Lyric

[Verse 1]

Pour another glass just to take the edge off,

The world's a little sharp, a little too defined.

This amber liquid sings a gentle lullaby,

A way to press the pause button in my mind.

It's comfort in the quiet, a friend on lonely nights,

Helps me talk a little louder, helps me find the lights.

[Chorus]

'Cause it's a good servant, a hand I can hold,

A way to unwind when the story gets old.

It's a whisper in the glass, a truth I can face,

A temporary refuge, a change of pace.

But it's a poor master, a shadow that grows,

A debt that you owe with every ounce that you pour.

It starts taking over till you can't be free—

Just a puppet on a string for all the world to see.

[Verse 2]

Woke up in the morning with a fog in my head,

Can't quite remember all the things that were said.

Another broken promise, another blurry line,

Lost the thread of thought, just passing through time.

Heated conversations that turn into a blur,

Chasing shadows in the dim light, no longer sure.

But the taste still lingers like a bittersweet kiss

In this dance with my demons—it's hard to miss.

[Chorus]

'Cause it's a good servant, a hand I can hold,

A way to unwind when the story gets old.

It's a whisper in the glass, a truth I can face,

A temporary refuge, a change of pace.

But it's a poor master, a shadow that grows,

A debt that you owe with every ounce that you pour.

It starts taking over till you can't be free—

Just a puppet on a string for all the world to see.

[Bridge]

I've danced in its rhythm, swayed to its tune,

In the glow of the bar lights, howling at the moon.

But when the dawn breaks and the light floods in,

I'm left with the echoes of where I've been.

So I take a deep breath and I count to ten,

Knowing I have to find my way back again.

[Chorus]

'Cause it's a good servant, a hand I can hold,

A way to unwind when the story gets old.

It's a whisper in the glass, a truth I can face,

A temporary refuge, a change of pace.

But it's a poor master, a shadow that grows,

A debt that you owe with every ounce that you pour.

It starts taking over till you can't be free—

Just a puppet on a string for all the world to see.

[Outro]

So I'll tread carefully on this winding road,

With each sip remember the weight of the load.

It serves me well yet pulls me down too fast—

In the end it's a dance I pray won't last.

6. Don't Let Those Words Define Who I Am

The Story of the Soul (The Why)

Inspiration: The devastating feeling of being entirely defined by a mistake, knowing my partner judged me by the hurtful messages rather than the positive, loving behaviour that came before. I felt a profound sense of injustice that her final view of me was limited to my worst moment.

What I Was Trying to Portray: I intended to communicate the desperate plea for self-justification and understanding. Because the song was never shared, I was using the rhetorical plea to her as a way to internally fight her definition of me. The song is my attempt to argue for my own worth—the "man that you loved, the one with a plan"—so that I could move toward forgiving myself.

The Intentional Feeling: I aimed to express the vulnerable, raw pain of being misunderstood at the moment of loss. The feeling I sought to capture in the chorus is the deep, internal wound that "What you think of me now, it cuts like a knife," acknowledging that her final judgement is the painful metric I must now live with.

The Principle of Respectful Space

My Core Intent: I believe it is fundamentally wrong to ask someone back. If there is any real attachment, they should hopefully reach out once they have processed their hurt. My decision not to share this heartfelt song reinforces my commitment to respecting her process and her agency.

I wrote the song not for her to hear, but for me to process my pain whilst giving her the necessary space to heal on her own terms.

The Story of the Craft (The How)

How I Chose to Portray It: I deliberately structured the song as a direct, final address to my partner, even though I knew I wouldn't send it. I used this intense, one-sided conversation to process the unfairness of the situation, contrasting the scale of our positive history with the single, singular act of my weakness.

The Chosen Focus: I focused on contrasting the magnitude of the positive with the isolation of the negative:

The Golden Past (Verse 1 & Bridge): I opened by invoking the memories of "laughter under skies so blue" and "late nights talking" to establish the solid foundation of love. I used the Bridge to argue for my worth, claiming that "Every laugh we shared, every tear that we cried" proves the relationship was real, and therefore, my true self is the one I want her to remember.

Minimising the Failure: In Verse 1, I framed the mistake as a tragic loss of control—a moment when I "let my guard down" and the words "slipped from my lips." My intention was to emphasise the unintended, instantaneous nature of the error, hoping that this framing would allow me to see it as an accident, not a reflection of my core being.

Creating the Distance (Verse 2): I used the imagery of her reaction—a "wall rise" in her eyes—to physically represent the emotional distance and the finality of the breakup. This visually communicates the helplessness I felt in watching the love come "undone."

The Lifeline (The Listen):
https://on.soundcloud.com/beFL6TFYX6cD8xL0X1

The Lyric

[Verse 1]

We shared our laughter under skies so blue,

Late nights talking 'bout dreams, just me and you.

But shadows crept in on that fateful night,

When I let my guard down, lost in the light.

A drink too many, my heart felt so free,

But words slipped from my lips, didn't mean to be mean.

You looked at me different, a spark turned to ash,

As I saw the trust fade, like a whispering flash.

[Chorus]

Oh, don't let those words define who I am,

The man that you loved, the one with a plan.

I gave you my all, my heart laid bare,

Yet now you reflect on my foolish despair.

What you think of me now, it cuts like a knife,

Those moments of weakness, they haunted my life.

[Verse 2]

We walked on the edge of love's gentle flame,

Hand in hand, through the joy, through the pain.

But echoes of laughter turned to whispers of doubt,

You shifting in silence, I could feel you pull out.

In the depth of your eyes, I saw a wall rise,

Each word of regret like a storm in disguise.

I tried to explain, but the damage was done,

The love we had slowly came undone.

[Chorus]

Oh, don't let those words define who I am,

The man that you loved, the one with a plan.

I gave you my all, my heart laid bare,

Yet now you reflect on my foolish despair.

What you think of me now, it cuts like a knife,

Those moments of weakness, they haunted my life.

[Bridge]

I can't erase the shadows of nights I regret,

But the person you knew is still here, don't forget.

Every laugh we shared, every tear that we cried,

Shows a love that was real, not a weakness we hide.

I wish you could see beyond the mistakes,

Because my heart still beats for all of your takes.

In the quiet of dusk, where our memories swayed,

Let the sunshine in, let love not fade.

[Chorus]

Oh, don't let those words define who I am,

The man that you loved, the one with a plan.

I gave you my all, my heart laid bare,

Yet now you reflect on my foolish despair.

What you think of me now, it cuts like a knife,

Those moments of weakness, they haunted my life.

[Outro]

So here we stand on this new, lonely road,

Trying to nurse the wounds, carry the load.

I hope you find clarity in time's gentle grace,

Because I'll always cherish the love we embraced.

Though it's hard to move on when your heart's in the dark,

Know that you were my light, my still, precious spark.

7. See Me!

The Story of the Soul (The Why)

Inspiration: The desire to revisit the theme from "Don't Let Those Words Define Who I Am," based on the principle that sometimes a lyric needs to be rewritten until the correct emotional argument emerges. The focus remains the rhetorical plea for my partner to see the fullness of my love and character, not just the single mistake.

What I Was Trying to Portray: I wanted to directly portray my confusion and pain over her selective memory. My intention was to ask: How can months of good behaviour, care, and connection be instantly eclipsed by a single error? The song is about pleading for recognition of the whole person, the man who still "would've given you everything."

The Intentional Feeling: I aimed for a feeling of vulnerable, heartbroken desperation mixed with confusion. The feeling is one of standing "unseen"—the man she loved is still present, but she is mentally trapped by the trauma of the "voice in the night."

The Principle of Respectful Space

My Core Intent: I believe it's wrong to demand someone return. If there is genuine attachment, she should reach out on her own timeline after processing the hurt. The lyric is not a demand sent to her, but an internal expression of my pain and my unwavering belief in the core of our relationship. I'm using the song to vent the argument I wish I could make whilst respecting her need for distance.

The Story of the Craft (The How)

How I Chose to Portray It: I structured this song to make clear the contrast between the past and the present more sharply than before, making the source of the conflict explicit: her fear versus my reality. I used softer, more romantic imagery in the verses, only to have the chorus brutally shatter that imagery.

The Chosen Focus: I focused on the difference between our two perspectives:

Establishing the Romantic High (Verse 1): I started with powerful, comforting imagery—"soft glow of the moonlit sky," love like a "lullaby," and dancing "until dawn"—to establish how high the stakes were. This makes the fall feel more tragic.

Focusing on Her Internal Conflict (Chorus): I made the central message about her perception. Phrases like "a voice in the night has filled you with fear" and "Now you're painting my soul with colours of the past" are used to define the problem as being rooted in her emotional response to the memory, not just my initial action.

The Plea for Wholeness (Verse 2 & Bridge): I used the rhetorical question, "How could you overlook all the smiles, the care?" to challenge the injustice of her selective focus. The Bridge is a direct emotional request—"Trapped in your head, whilst I stand here unseen"—which perfectly encapsulates my core desire for her to look past the shadows and truly see me again.

The Lifeline (The Listen):

https://on.soundcloud.com/dQL9C2zDEysm4pH1wC

The Lyric

[Verse 1]

Underneath the soft glow of the moonlit sky,

I thought we had it all, love like a lullaby.

But whispers in the dark took you by surprise,

Moments lost in laughter turned to echoes, now I sigh.

Remember the nights we danced until dawn?

Each touch felt electric, but now it feels wrong.

A heart once so open, now caught in the grind,

You bring up the shadows that chill in your mind.

[Chorus]

And I would've given you everything, my dear,

But a voice in the night has filled you with fear.

Thought you knew me well, thought love would last,

Now you're painting my soul with colours of the past.

The words spoken lightly, in a moment of cheer,

Are haunting your heart, turning love to despair.

[Verse 2]

I see you frowning, the spark in your eyes dimmed,

Once filled with brightness, now feels like a sin.

That night of mistakes, just a moment of pride,

Yet here we are now, with your heart full of doubt inside.

How could you overlook all the smiles, the care?

The love that we built, like castles in air.

Every promise I made, they danced on the breeze,

But now they're just whispers that bring you to your knees.

[Chorus]

And I would've given you everything, my dear,

But a voice in the night has filled you with fear.

Thought you knew me well, thought love would last,

Now you're painting my soul with colours of the past.

The words spoken lightly, in a moment of cheer,

Are haunting your heart, turning love to despair.

[Bridge]

I'd lay my soul bare to erase this dark stain,

If only you'd hold me through the joy and the pain.

But echoes keep ringing in the silence between,

Trapped in your head, whilst I stand here unseen.

Let's look past the shadows, the stormy weather,

Find the shining heart from the love we tethered.

If you could just see through the hurt and the tears,

You'd find I'm still with you, embracing the years.

[Outro]

So here's my heart, waiting under the stars,

Hoping you'll see me, despite all the scars.

Let the echoes fade softly, return to the light,

Let's rewrite our story, together, and right.

With every beat of my heart, I'll keep loving you near,

Let's silence the echoes and bring back the cheer.

8. The Unfinished Embrace

The Story of the Soul (The Why)

Inspiration: The central irony of my partner's emotional vulnerability: She has strong emotional defences, dislikes cuddling or easy physical closeness, and finds attachment difficult, yet her passionate late-night painting sessions exclusively result in art depicting couples embracing.

What I Was Trying to Portray: I intended to portray her internal conflict with deep empathy. The song is my way of articulating the painful disconnect between her conscious defence mechanisms and her unconscious, desperate need for intimacy. I wanted to show the listener that her standoffishness isn't a lack of love, but a "prison" built from past hurt.

The Intentional Feeling: I aimed to convey a feeling of observational tenderness and knowing sadness. The emotion is defined by the central image of the "unfinished embrace"— the perfect love she can create and express on canvas but is "terrified to know" in real life.

The Principle of Respectful Space

My Core Intent: This song is a quiet act of understanding her reality, not a demand for her to change. By focusing on her internal life, I am respecting the validity of her defences, even as I recognise the tragic irony of her art. I am processing my realisation that the distance is a consequence of her past and her emotional process, allowing me to be patient and non-judgemental towards her need for space.

The Story of the Craft (The How)

How I Chose to Portray It: I used the canvas and brushstrokes as the primary narrative device—her art literally becomes the "confession" that her words cannot make. The structure contrasts her physical setting (the solitary studio) with the emotional content of her work (the entwined figures).

The Chosen Focus: I focused on specific artistic and emotional metaphors:

Art as Confession (Chorus): I made the Chorus the centrepiece, explicitly defining the art as the emotional truth she cannot speak: "Her art is a confession, a story left untold." This tells the listener that the secret to her heart isn't hidden; it's right there, visible in her work.

Physical vs. Emotional Distance (Verse 1 & 2): I established the physical setup of her solitude ("In the dim light of her studio") and then immediately contrasted it with the longing found in the pictures, where figures are "entwined in gentle grace." The "walls built high around her" are the safety net she relies on, but the art proves the desire is still there.

The Language of Colour (Bridge): I elevated the painting process, describing the brushstrokes as a "language" and the colours as telling a "secret." This choice demonstrates that her true spirit ("igniting her own spark") is expressed through this protected medium, which is safer than expressing the longing directly to a partner.

The Lifeline (The Listen):

https://on.soundcloud.com/MrNokYyFGPT9XRk2K4

The Lyric

[Verse 1]

In the dim light of her studio, where shadows softly play,

She dances with her brushes, letting colours lead the way.

Building worlds on canvas, she finds solace in her art,

Each stroke, a quiet heartbeat, a window to her heart.

The people in her pictures, entwined in gentle grace,

A perfect kind of comfort, a longing to embrace.

[Chorus]

Her art is a confession, a story left untold,

A longing and a prison, a truth she can't uphold.

She paints the closeness that her heart is terrified to know,

An unfinished embrace, where silent sorrows flow.

[Verse 2]

She faces her reflection, with tears that won't run dry,

The lines upon the canvas speak of love she can't deny.

Wounds from days of laughter, now whispering regret,

Walls built high around her, a safety net she's set.

In every painted figure, their hands are strong and tight,

A promise made in silence, beneath the moonlit night.

[Chorus]

Her art is a confession, a story left untold,

A longing and a prison, a truth she can't uphold.

She paints the closeness that her heart is terrified to know,

An unfinished embrace, where silent sorrows flow.

[Bridge]

The brushstrokes are a language, a whisper in the dark,

Each colour tells a secret, igniting her own spark.

A testament to courage, in every hue and shade,

A hope that lingers softly, where fears are unafraid.

But still she feels the distance, an ache that won't subside,

Caught between the longing and the love she must abide.

[Verse 3]

Through the layers of her canvas, she pours her soul and pride,

Seeking connections lost, whilst keeping pain inside.

Creating beautiful illusions, of laughs that fill the air,

Yet afraid to reach for someone, the fear she'll find them there.

So in her quiet moments, she finds strength in the night,

An unfinished embrace, where shadows meet the light.

[Chorus]

Her art is a confession, a story left untold,

A longing and a prison, a truth she can't uphold.

She paints the closeness that her heart is terrified to know,

An unfinished embrace, where silent sorrows flow.

[Outro]

As she lifts her brush to canvas, her heart begins to soar,

In every stroke of passion, she's finding more and more.

A journey of creation, of love that's yet to bloom,

In the unfinished embrace, she'll carve away the gloom.

Her canvases will tell it, a tale of hope and grace,

Through the colours of her longing, she'll finally find her place.

9. Where Do You Go From Here?

The Story of the Soul (The Why)

Inspiration: The experience of a friend losing their job, resonating with my own past experiences of losing a partner and facing redundancy. I recognised the shared emotional aftershock and the profound uncertainty that follows such life-changing events.

What I Was Trying to Portray: My intention was to articulate that the immediate aftermath of a sudden loss is characterised by a "silent aftershock"—a state of disorientation, where the familiar world has crumbled without a loud crash. I wanted to show the shift from panicked fear to the courageous acceptance that the loss mandates a complete self-reinvention.

The Intentional Feeling: I aimed to convey a feeling of vulnerable disorientation that evolves into resolute hope. The feeling moves from the "unstable ground" of the verses to the energised, proactive question, "Where do you go from here?"

The Principle of Respectful Space

My Core Intent: Whilst the primary loss in this song is external (a job), the emotional landscape is similar to the loss of a partner. I am using the reflection on uncertainty to process my own need to move forward. The resolution in the outro—"I'll keep moving forward, I'm ready to fight"—is a promise to myself to evolve, without needing to pressure or wait for the other person involved in a past loss to make their move. I am defining my new path independently.

The Story of the Craft (The How)

How I Chose to Portray It: I deliberately used metaphors of structure and foundation to show the chaos of the change. The song is structured as a moment-by-moment process, moving from the sudden shock (Verse 1) to the hesitant questioning (Verse 2), and finally to a recognition of responsibility (Bridge).

The Chosen Focus: I focused on specific imagery to communicate the nature of the change:

The Silent Disruption (Verse 1 & Chorus): I used the phrase "The title changed, didn't make a sound" and "silent aftershock" to highlight that the deepest life changes often happen quietly, forcing an internal crisis rather than an external one. The old path vanished behind a "silent curtain drop."

The Weight of Expectation (Bridge): The Bridge intentionally shifts the focus from personal loss to the burden of others' needs. When I sing, "all the hands that reach for mine, expecting me to lead," I'm portraying the complex reality that my own grief is compounded by the responsibility

I feel towards others, adding a "heavy cost" to my uncertainty.

Finding Clarity in Chaos (Chorus & Outro): I framed the uncertainty as the birthplace of opportunity: the "different rhythm" and "brand new point of view." The ultimate rhetorical question, "Where do you go from here," becomes an empowering call to action, transforming fear into the resolve to "keep moving forward."

The Lifeline (The Listen):
https://on.soundcloud.com/9vx9xUQsf4wnrSIUO2

The Lyric

[Verse 1]

The title changed, didn't make a sound,

Felt my whole life shifting on unstable ground.

The future I was certain of, just went unseen,

A silent curtain drop on a familiar scene.

Thought I knew my path, every twist and turn,

Now I find myself in a world where I yearn.

With echoes of memories, haunting my mind,

I'm searching for solace, a way to unwind.

[Chorus]

And the ground beneath my feet, it feels so new,

A different rhythm, a brand new point of view.

It's the silent aftershock, the sudden, gentle hum,

A new story starting, after the old one's done.

A spark ignites the shadows that linger around,

In this quiet moment, I'm lost then found.

[Verse 2]

Time's got a way of changing everything,

As the clock ticks softly, hear the heartstrings sing.

The dreams that were held so close to my chest,

Now tangle with questions I cannot suppress.

What if I take the chance, and leap into the blue?

What if this undefined path leads me to the truth?

With every whispered breath, I gather my strength,

This journey beckons me to go to great lengths.

[Chorus]

And the ground beneath my feet, it feels so new,

A different rhythm, a brand new point of view.

It's the silent aftershock, the sudden, gentle hum,

A new story starting, after the old one's done.

A spark ignites the shadows that linger around,

In this quiet moment, I'm lost then found.

[Bridge]

And all the hands that reach for mine, expecting me to lead,

I feel the weight of every single need.

A different kind of burden, a silent, heavy cost,

The fear of being the reason something precious is lost.

With every tear I've shed, strengthen my resolve,

In this sea of uncertainty, I must evolve.

[Chorus]

And the ground beneath my feet, it feels so new,

A different rhythm, a brand new point of view.

It's the silent aftershock, the sudden, gentle hum,

A new story starting, after the old one's done.

A spark ignites the shadows that linger around,

In this quiet moment, I'm lost then found.

[Outro]

Where do you go from here? Where do you go from here?

When the road ahead is anything but clear.

A brand new start, a brand new page,

Stepping out of the past and onto a new stage.

As the echoes of yesterday fade into the night,

I'll keep moving forward, I'm ready to fight.

Part II: The Rebuilding and the Anchors (Songs 10-17)

The slow, deliberate work of healing, establishing boundaries, reconnecting with self-worth, and finding healthy support.

10. I am the Road

The Story of the Soul (The Why)

Inspiration: The relentless and overwhelming financial pressure of being the sole earner supporting three households, where unexpected costs were always appearing. I recognised that I could only do so much and desperately needed a cathartic lyric to express that I have limits.

What I Was Trying to Portray: My core intention was to define a healthy boundary using the analogy of a road. I wanted to clearly state: "I am your solid support and foundation, but I am not the ultimate source of control." The road analogy allows me to accept my role as a supportive guide without taking responsibility for the outside factors (the weather) or the choices of others (the car).

The Intentional Feeling: I aimed to convey a feeling of weary, yet resolute commitment. The song is an emotional release of the burden, finding peace by accepting my powerful, yet limited, role as the "silent, loving guide."

The Principle of Respectful Space

My Core Intent: This song is a declaration of self-

63

preservation and healthy boundaries. By defining myself as the road, I am respecting the agency of others—they are the "car you drive" and must make their own decisions about "how they move forwards." The lyric provides support but refuses to accept responsibility for their choices or for circumstances outside of my control, like the unpredictable "potholes" caused by my past or external pressures.

The Story of the Craft (The How)

How I Chose to Portray It: I built the entire narrative around the central, sustained metaphor of the road, contrasting its enduring nature with the unpredictable elements it encounters. The song speaks directly from the perspective of this foundation.

The Chosen Focus: I focused on contrasting my physical commitment with my emotional limitations:

The Act of Foundation (Verse 1): I began by describing the immense personal sacrifice required to become the foundation: transforming from a "jagged, lonely piece" of "river rock" into the smooth surface. This establishes the deliberate, painful effort behind the support I provide.

Defining the Boundary (Chorus): The Chorus is the central declaration of the song. By stating definitively, "I am not the car you drive, not the rain or sun," I am explicitly drawing the line between what I am (the path) and what I am not (the choices and the unpredictable environment). The "smoothness of the asphalt" represents the best I can offer, which is tied to my limited capacity.

Acknowledging Imperfection (Verse 2): I integrated the self-doubt by acknowledging that my own past "weakness" or "fracture" sometimes manifests as a "sudden pothole." This grounds the metaphor, showing that even the foundation I lay is imperfect, which reinforces the message that my performance is not always within my control.

The Enduring Promise (Bridge & Outro): Despite the challenges, the Bridge reaffirms the silent commitment to "keep the surface level," providing a steadfast, unwavering presence for their journeys.

The Lifeline (The Listen):
https://on.soundcloud.com/goauWND8kj008KIb0U

The Lyric

[Verse 1]

I started out as river rock, a jagged, lonely piece,

But for the ones I cherished, my brokenness would cease.

I hammered down the ridges, I laid the asphalt low,

A foundation for the footsteps of those I'd watch them go.

[Chorus]

I am not the car you drive, not the rain or sun,

I'm just the path beneath you 'til your journey's run.

The smoothness of the asphalt, the cracks you bear,

Are all the care I could give, and all I had to share.

[Verse 2]

Sometimes the way is easy, a surface clean and fast,

A welcome that is solid, a moment built to last.

But other times a weakness, a fracture from my past,

Becomes a sudden pothole, a shadow quickly cast.

[Chorus]

I am not the car you drive, not the rain or sun,

I'm just the path beneath you 'til your journey's run.

The smoothness of the asphalt, the cracks you bear,

Are all the care I could give, and all I had to share.

[Bridge]

So I'll keep the surface level, I'll sweep away the stones,

My silent, steadfast promise, the ground they've always

known.

Every footprint left behind, every tear and joy,

I hold their tales so gently, each girl and every boy.

[Verse 3]

In the dusk of evening, where the shadows start to blend,

I carry every secret, every smile, every friend.

When the morning sun breaks free, painting gold on each

lane, I witness all the stories, the pleasure and the pain.

[Chorus]

I am not the car you drive, not the rain or sun,

I'm just the path beneath you 'til your journey's run.

The smoothness of the asphalt, the cracks you bear,

Are all the care I could give, and all I had to share.

[Outro]

So here I stand, unwavering, under weight and weathered

skies, A testament to journeys, where the spirit never dies.

I am but a humble road, a silent, loving guide,

As you traverse the distance, take me with you on your ride.

11. The Forge

The Story of the Soul (The Why)

Inspiration: The deep regret I now feel about raising my sons to be "strong," influenced by my military background. I believed toughness was the right path, but I now mourn the loss of a closer, more loving, and emotionally connected relationship with them during their childhood. Though we have a good relationship now, the pain of those lost moments does not lessen.

What I Was Trying to Portray: I intended to portray the tragedy of good intentions gone wrong. My love was never absent—it was simply misapplied, manifesting as a "hammer" instead of an embrace. The core message is the painful realisation that whilst I succeeded in creating "warriors," I sacrificed emotional closeness and vulnerability along the way.

The Intentional Feeling: I aimed to convey a feeling of profound, aching regret and confession. The tone is deeply self-critical, using the vivid, industrial imagery of the forge to describe the sterile, hard process I chose instead of the "simple" sweetness of fatherhood.

The Principle of Respectful Space

My Core Intent: This lyric is a private acknowledgement of my own failure, not a plea for my sons to absolve me. I am defining and owning my responsibility for the emotional distance of the past. By articulating this regret within the song, I am processing the grief of those lost moments, which allows me to be a better, more emotionally present father now without putting the burden of my past choices on my sons.

The Story of the Craft (The How)

How I Chose to Portray It: I used the sustained, powerful metaphor of the Blacksmith's Forge to describe the parenting process. I defined the key players: I am the hammer/chisel/forge, and my sons are the iron ore. The lyrics contrast the destructive nature of the tools with the loving intent behind their use.

The Chosen Focus: I focused on contrasting the tools of strength with the language of softness:

The Flawed Process (Verse 1 & 2): I established that my love became the "hammer," and my goal was to "hammer down the soft spots" to make them immune to hurt. This illustrates the flaw in my protective philosophy, leading to the creation of a "hollow space" where a softer, more emotionally available man could have been.

The Refrain of Redemption: The Refrain serves as the central moment of clarity, articulating the exact lesson I failed to teach: not how to fight, but "how to let them go" and embrace a "kinder state of mind." It is the wish to go back and replace the lessons of steel with lessons of grace.

The Trade (Bridge): The Bridge offers the ultimate emotional summation of my regret.

I explicitly state that the external measure of success (the "trophy" and "grand display") is worthless compared to the simple, loving connection of "your small hand in my hand," effectively dissolving the forge metaphor and replacing it with pure, simple affection.

The Lifeline (The Listen):
https://on.soundcloud.com/SloEb8DufydkNOxXu6

The Lyric

[Verse 1]

I saw the world as fire, bright and wild,

You were the iron ore, my precious child,

My love became the hammer, shaping you strong,

Moulding every curve, righting every wrong.

I hammered down the soft spots, made you tough and lean,

So no one could ever hurt you, or see what was unseen.

[Chorus]

In the forge of my heart, where the flames dance high,

I crafted every moment, under the endless sky,

But the tools that were for greatness brought shadows to

dwell,For the memories that haunt me, they're the tales I

cannot tell.

[Verse 2]

I made you hard and polished, a warrior's will of steel,

But in the heat of the battle, it's my heart that feels,

My love was like a chisel, carving you from stone,

Yet I left a hollow space, a softer man's unknown.

[Refrain]

The world you've faced is harder than I thought you'd find,

I wish I taught you different, a kinder state of mind,

Not how to fight the battles, but how to let them go,

To chase the dreams that linger, in the gentle afterglow.

[Verse 3]

I gave you every lesson, every step I thought was right,

But the weight of every struggle, it keeps you up at night.

And every hard-earned victory, it carries such a price,

For the forge can build a man, but love can roll the dice.

[Chorus]

In the forge of my heart, where the flames dance high,

I crafted every moment, under the endless sky,

But the tools that were for greatness brought shadows to

dwell, For the memories that haunt me, they're the tales I

cannot tell.

[Bridge]

Oh, I'd trade every trophy, every grand display,

Just to be a simple father, watching you at play,

With your small hand in my hand, I'd lead you through the

day, Teaching you the sweetness of life in every way.

[Verse 4]

So let the world keep turning, and let the fires blaze,

For in the warmth of love, our spirits will amaze,

I'll hold you close forever, through all of life's demands,

And together we'll uncover, the beauty of our hands.

[Outro]

In the ashes of the forge, there's a lesson yet to share,

That love can leave you stronger, when you know how much

we care, So take the world on boldly, but remember, child of

mine, You're not alone in battle, with my heart and yours

entwined.

12. Flame of Hope

The Story of the Soul (The Why)

Inspiration: A musing on the fragile nature of hope and the belief that hope is not always a random, passive gift. This was solidified by my memory of building and tending a fire whilst camping, where success depends on both uncontrollable factors (weather, wood) and personal effort, capability, and commitment.

What I Was Trying to Portray: My intention was to communicate that true, lasting hope requires active maintenance and stubborn will. The song is an argument against fatalism, stating that one's commitment to the effort is just as vital as the kindling. I wanted to show that the small, personal act of tending the flame (hope) can be a guiding force against overwhelming darkness.

The Intentional Feeling: I aimed to convey a feeling of resilient defiance and quiet solitude. The emotion is one of focused determination—crouching in the darkness, personally fighting the elements to keep a vital internal light burning.

The Principle of Respectful Space

My Core Intent: This lyric is a declaration of self-reliance and internal strength. By focusing the entire song on my effort—"my own stubborn will," "my own burning"—I am asserting my capacity to heal and move forward independently. I don't need external validation or help to find the "compass"; the process of building hope is a solitary, self-guided journey, allowing me to fully respect the space and time of others.

The Story of the Craft (The How)

How I Chose to Portray It: I used the sustained, powerful metaphor of the campfire to represent the state of hope, with the surrounding darkness and weather representing external struggles. The narrative is structured around the practical steps of building and sustaining the fire.

The Chosen Focus: I focused on contrasting the external forces of destruction with the internal forces of will:

Active Creation (Verse 1): I started by defining the challenge: beginning with "nothing, just the dirt" whilst others may have easier lives. This immediately establishes that my hope (the flame) is earned through personal effort—finding the "piece of pine" and physically "feeding the flickering flame."

The Storm of Doubt (Verse 2): I personified the external forces as conscious threats: the wind is a "breath that tries to kill" the fragile flame of hope. This makes the fight feel immediate and existential, highlighting the power of my "own stubborn will" to overcome it.

Personal Ownership (Bridge & Verse 3): The Bridge asserts ownership: "this is my own burning, the hope I've carried down." In Verse 3, I emphasised the solitude and intimacy of the act: the fire "needs no other witness" and is "all that's left of me," making the maintenance of hope a deeply personal act of courage.

The Lifeline (The Listen):
https://on.soundcloud.com/O0GNcHfArsHfpMhAIu

The Lyric

[Verse 1]

Some are given kindling, a stack of bone-dry wood,

Whilst I began with nothing, just the dirt where I stood.

But then I found a piece of pine, a handful of grace,

To give this fragile burning, a solid, hopeful place.

So I crouch here in the black night, with my hands against the

stone, Feeding the flickering flame, I refuse to be alone.

[Chorus]

Oh, the flame of hope, it dances in the dark,

A light that keeps on shining, igniting every spark.

No matter how the storm rages, or the shadows try to creep,

This fire keeps on burning, my heart, it will not sleep.

[Verse 2]

The storm has its own language, a voice that wants to cease,

This tender, fragile burning, would love to find release.

The wind comes in a shiver, a breath that tries to kill,

But it won't be the master of my own stubborn will.

I wrap my dreams around it, like a blanket made of love,

This flicker is my compass, guiding me from above.

[Chorus]

Oh, the flame of hope, it dances in the dark,

A light that keeps on shining, igniting every spark.

No matter how the storm rages, or the shadows try to creep,

This fire keeps on burning, my heart, it will not sleep.

[Bridge]

The winds may take the ashes, the rain may try to drown,

But this is my own burning, the hope I've carried down.

With every match I strike, I'm lighting pathways back,

To the joy and the laughter, that fills this empty track.

[Verse 3]

In the quiet of the evening, when the world begins to fade,

I'll gather 'round my fire, and let my soul cascade.

For it needs no other witness, no one else to see,

This small, quiet fire is all that's left of me.

I'll sing my song of courage, in every whispered tone,

With the flame of love beside me, I'll never be alone.

[Chorus]

Oh, the flame of hope, it dances in the dark,

A light that keeps on shining, igniting every spark.

No matter how the storm rages, or the shadows try to creep,

This fire keeps on burning, my heart, it will not sleep.

[Outro]

So let it flicker brightly, let it light the way ahead,

With the flame of hope beside me, I have a life to lead. 0

Through the hard times and the struggles, my spirit refuses to bend,

For within this burning ember, I know my heart will mend.

13. Quiet Moments

The Story of the Soul (The Why)

Inspiration: The simple, seemingly insignificant, yet deeply meaningful moments of my partner's presence at home. These are the instinctive, unthinking acts—the small smile when catching my eye, or the way she curls into me at night—that affirm the depth of our connection.

What I Was Trying to Portray: I intended to communicate that the most powerful, indisputable proof of love lies in these unconscious, natural behaviours. The song is a celebration of the simple joy of domestic life, arguing that these moments of "quiet art" are more valuable and reassuring than any planned declaration.

The Intentional Feeling: I aimed to convey a feeling of deep contentment, security, and gratitude. The emotion is one of peaceful certainty, where all doubts disappear because the body language is honest, instinctive, and true.

The Principle of Respectful Space

My Core Intent: This song is my internal acknowledgement that a relationship's strength is built on mutual, unforced comfort. By celebrating the love that "a mind can't plot" and the "instinct" of her gestures, I am affirming that true connection is organic and spontaneous. I find immense peace in knowing that her affection is not a choice she has to think about, but a natural reaction, which requires no demanding or seeking on my part.

The Story of the Craft (The How)

How I Chose to Portray It: I structured the song around a chronology of daily intimacy, moving from the moment of recognition (watching her read) to the comfort of night (curling into me) and the quiet start of the morning (coffee and talk). The entire focus is on small, observable actions.

The Chosen Focus: I focused on elevating the "insignificant" actions to be the most meaningful:

The Unconscious Proof (Verse 1 & Chorus): I used specific, gentle actions—the "little smile," the way she "curls into me"—to establish the core idea. The Chorus then explicitly states my thesis: "The way that you find me without a thought" is the "proof that I need," positioning instinct over calculated effort.

Creating Sanctuary (Verse 2): I established the domestic setting as a sacred space—a "sanctuary of ours"—where the external world "fades away." This reinforces that these quiet moments create a unique, shared world where our "spirits can fly."

Treasuring the Moment (Bridge): The Bridge elevates these small moments to high value, calling them "treasures of gold." This shows my commitment to actively appreciating the present and using her simple presence to dispel all "gloom," making her touch the ultimate source of safety and security.

The Lifeline (The Listen):
https://on.soundcloud.com/FSlSbeb8gS38YFaj9y

The Lyric

[Verse 1]

I was just sitting here, watching you read,

You look up for a second, a moment indeed.

And you catch my eye, just a little smile,

Like you're happy I'm here for a little while.

And then later at night, when the day is done,

The way you curl into me, my only one.

It's not something you think about, I can tell,

Just an instinct, a kind of beautiful spell.

[Chorus]

And it's these little moments that mean the most,

The small, simple things, how we get close.

The way that you find me without a thought,

All the love in the world that a mind can't plot.

It's the natural way you just pull me near,

All the proof that I need, all my doubts disappear.

It's more than a feeling, it's a simple, quiet art,

The way that you reach for me and steal my heart.

[Verse 2]

In the soft morning light, when you glance my way,

The warmth in your gaze, it brightens my day.

With coffee brewing, the world fades away,

In this sanctuary of ours, where love leads the way.

We talk about dreams, we laugh and we sigh,

In the silence between, our spirits can fly.

I hold onto every shared glance and sigh,

For in those quiet moments, our love learns to fly.

[Chorus]

And it's these little moments that mean the most,

The small, simple things, how we get close.

The way that you find me without a thought,

All the love in the world that a mind can't plot.

It's the natural way you just pull me near,

All the proof that I need, all my doubts disappear.

It's more than a feeling, it's a simple, quiet art,

The way that you reach for me and steal my heart.

[Bridge]

When storms roll through, and the shadows loom,

Your hand in mine dispels all the gloom.

In every tender touch, in every shared sigh,

I find my forever with you standing by.

So let's hold these moments, like treasures of gold,

For in the quiet evenings, love stories unfold.

We'll weave every whisper into the night's glow,

In these tranquil hours, our love will just grow.

[Outro]

So here's to the silence that speaks so loud,

To the moments together that make us proud.

In the echoes of laughter, in the calm of the sea,

It's these quiet moments that mean everything to me.

14. The Wonder Years

The Story of the Soul (The Why)

Inspiration: The realisation that when asked what I truly wanted for dinner, I had no real desire or want for anything in particular. This sparked a deep yearning to recapture the wide-eyed, automatic excitement children feel about everything, a joy that seems to fade as adult concerns take over.

What I Was Trying to Portray: I intended to communicate the tragedy of lost enthusiasm—the moment a person realises that life has dampened their capacity for simple wonder. The song is a journey back through specific, vivid childhood memories to identify what was lost: the "flutter in the stomach" and the "simple magic hanging in the air."

The Intentional Feeling: I aimed to convey a feeling of deep nostalgia mixed with gentle resolve. The initial feeling is one of longing and loss ("Where did it go?"), but it evolves into a promise to actively seek out and preserve those simple joys in the future.

The Principle of Respectful Space

My Core Intent: This lyric is a completely internal reflection on my personal emotional state and life history. I am processing the effects of time and stress on my own capacity for joy. By focusing on my own lack of desire and my quest to reignite the "wide-eyed stare," I am charting a path towards emotional healing that is entirely self-contained and independent of external relationships.

The Story of the Craft (The How)

How I Chose to Portray It: I used a structure based on a rapid-fire succession of vivid, sensory childhood images (Verse 1 and 2), contrasting this richness with the generalised, abstract lack of feeling in the Chorus. The memories are the "proof" of the joy that was once possible.

The Chosen Focus: I focused on elevating the smallest, most immediate joys:

Sensory Specificity (Verse 1): I made the memories tangible: "scraped-up knees," the "melty prize" of a chocolate chip, the "firefly." These are small, immediate rewards that require no complex planning or purchase, emphasising how easily wonder was achieved.

The Biological Response (Chorus): I defined the lost feeling in clear physical terms: a "flutter in the stomach" and a "tickle in the chest." By defining joy as a primal, physical reaction that existed "Before the world had put my heart to the test," I emphasise that the loss is a consequence of experience and time.

The Call to Reclamation (Bridge & Outro): The Bridge moves from memory to action. It is the crucial pivot where I resolve to "pause and breathe" and "take the pledge" to "seek out joy in the smallest things." The Outro softens the loss, suggesting that the wonder isn't truly gone, but just "tucked away," ready to be found again through conscious effort.

The Lifeline (The Listen):
https://on.soundcloud.com/jRyhrOM3sFJRk9hOhz

The Lyric

[Verse 1]

Sun-bleached streets and scraped-up knees,

A brand-new bike, a gentle breeze.

The final bell, a hopeful sound,

Summer's waiting, all around.

The chocolate chip, a melty prize,

Reflected in my eager eyes.

A birthday cake with candles bright,

A firefly in the coming night.

Oh, that feeling, light and fast,

A joy I hoped would always last.

[Chorus]

A flutter in the stomach, a tickle in the chest,

Before the world had put my heart to the test.

A million little wonders, a universe of bright,

Where every tiny spark was a source of light.

Where did it go? The wide-eyed stare?

The simple magic hanging in the air?

The butterflies that used to fly,

As time went on, and passed me by.

[Verse 2]

Crickets sing under starlit skies,

With shadows dancing, the night complies.

Treehouse dreams and whispered schemes,

Hiding from the world, lost in our dreams.

Waves of laughter, friends all near,

In those moments, the sky was clear.

Playing until the dark would fall,

The enchantment wrapped around us all.

[Chorus]

A flutter in the stomach, a tickle in the chest,

Before the world had put my heart to the test.

A million little wonders, a universe of bright,

Where every tiny spark was a source of light.

Where did it go? The wide-eyed stare?

The simple magic hanging in the air?

The butterflies that used to fly,

As time went on, and passed me by.

[Bridge]

Now the days are filled with rush and race,

But in the quiet, I find a trace.

Of that child within, waiting to play,

In the rhythm of life, it yearns to stay.

So I'll pause and breathe, near the world's edge,

To find the wonder, take the pledge.

To seek out joy in the smallest things,

Remembering the happiness each moment brings.

[Chorus]

A flutter in the stomach, a tickle in the chest,

Before the world had put my heart to the test.

A million little wonders, a universe of bright,

Where every tiny spark was a source of light.

Where did it go? The wide-eyed stare?

The simple magic hanging in the air?

The butterflies that used to fly,

As time went on, and passed me by.

[Outro]

Maybe it's not gone, just tucked away,

Waiting for a moment, a different day.

To find a small and simple thing,

And feel the joy that it can bring.

To find a single firefly,

And watch the magic, as it flies by.

15. The Wonder of my Days

The Story of the Soul (The Why)

Inspiration: The total, life-changing impact my partner had on me. She "burst through my life like a comet," making me the happiest I'd ever been. I wanted to capture the feeling that everything about her—even the way she simply moved or the small details of her presence—was an incredible, simple wonder.

What I Was Trying to Portray: I intended to communicate a love that is based on absolute and complete appreciation. The song is a catalogue of admiration, where I elevate every tiny, mundane detail into a profound miracle. I wanted the listener to understand that her "kind and fearless spirit" is what took my world from being fractured to being whole.

The Intentional Feeling: I aimed to convey a feeling of overwhelming awe, gratitude, and comfort. The central emotion is peaceful devotion, finding the "comfort in my heart" by simply observing her existence.

The Principle of Respectful Space

My Core Intent: This lyric is a celebration of my partner's influence on my life. It is an internal expression of gratitude for the transformation she sparked. By recognising her as my "sweetest guide," I affirm the immense space she took up in my life, and the lasting self-improvement she inspired, without making any demands on her. I am simply acknowledging the depth of my commitment to always "choose you."

The Story of the Craft (The How)

How I Chose to Portray It: I used a structure that moves from micro-observation (watching her play with her hair) to macro-

93

impact (making my world whole). The verses focus on physical details and deeds, whilst the chorus extracts the spiritual and emotional essence of her character.

The Chosen Focus: I focused on elevating simple actions into spiritual revelations:

The Wonder of Movement (Chorus): I made the physical aspects of her being—"how you move" and "the way your smile begins"—the central feature of the Chorus. This emphasises that her very existence and natural state are the source of my wonder.

Love as Action (Verse 2): I moved beyond passive beauty to active love. I transformed domestic tasks into profound emotional deeds: she doesn't just "clean the floors," she is "building a life for us to walk into." This shows my deep appreciation for how her love is put into practice through daily service and care.

The Colour Motif (Bridge): I deliberately used the motif of colour once more—"You've painted colour in my life, so vibrant and so bright"—to connect her artistic spirit to the emotional transformation I experienced. This powerful imagery links her passion directly to my joy.

The Final Vow (Outro): The Outro serves as the ultimate statement of unwavering loyalty, cementing the feeling that with her, I have found my "everything," and my commitment will not fade as the "seasons slip away."

The Lifeline (The Listen):
https://on.soundcloud.com/ao30aOzlbEoo2M77C3

The Lyric

[Verse 1]

I watched you sitting there reading,

Doing that thing, playing with your hair.

I felt that warmth inside me,

The comfort of you being there.

You seemed to sense me,

Looked up and gave me a smile.

Everything about you is a wonder,

A simple miracle for a little while.

[Chorus]

I'm watching how you move, it's everything to me,

And the way your smile begins, is a beautiful thing to see.

There's a whisper in your scent, a story in your soul,

And your kind and fearless spirit, is what makes my world whole.

You're just so incredible,

In all these simple ways.

You're the comfort in my heart,

The wonder of my days.

[Verse 2]

I see you try so hard, to give us all your best,

The simple way you feed me, puts my anxious heart to rest.

And it's more than just a recipe, a comfort deep and true,

And you don't just clean the floors, you're building a life for us to walk into.

You put your love in every deed,

A beautiful display,

And every little thing you do,

Just brightens up my day.

[Chorus]

I'm watching how you move, it's everything to me,

And the way your smile begins, is a beautiful thing to see.

There's a whisper in your scent, a story in your soul,

And your kind and fearless spirit, is what makes my world whole.

You're just so incredible,

In all these simple ways.

You're the comfort in my heart,

The wonder of my days.

[Bridge]

I see us growing old together, hand in hand through time,

Each moment treasured deeper, with a love that feels sublime.

You've painted colour in my life, so vibrant and so bright,

With you, the days are endless, beneath the stars and light.

[Verse 3]

Through every laugh and tear we've shared, you stand right by my

side, In all of life's uncertainties, you've been my sweetest guide.

So here's to every little thing, that makes me smile each day, I

'll cherish you forever, as the seasons slip away.

[Outro]

So let the world keep turning, and let the stars align,

With you, I've found my everything, forever you are mine.

In every corner of my heart, you've carved your place so true,

You're my joy, my peace, my love, In every moment, I'll choose

you.

16. Those Like Us

The Story of the Soul (The Why)

Inspiration: A conversation about the definition of friendship, contrasting the low-stakes, social definition popular in the village with the high-stakes, unspoken code I know from my military background. The conversation—where I noted no one checked on me despite my absence from the pub—highlighted the difference. The core phrase is the traditional toast: "To us and those like us, damned few."

What I Was Trying to Portray: I intended to articulate that true friendship is defined by a shared experience of fire or combat and the resulting unspoken commitment. The song is an argument that the "code that was written" in hardship is superior to the "surface-level handshake" of casual acquaintance. It's about being seen and understood without having to ask.

The Intentional Feeling: I aimed to convey a feeling of fierce loyalty, proud isolation, and deep, silent gratitude. The emotion is one of unapologetic conviction that deep connection is rare and priceless.

The Principle of Respectful Space

My Core Intent: This lyric is a clear boundary statement. I am defining the kind of connection I value and, by extension, respecting my own need for authentic, deep loyalty rather than shallow social interaction. I accept that others in the village may not understand my definition of "friend," and I respect their space by not demanding their superficial attention. I only need the few who hear the "silent call" and respect my space until I need them in the "zero-hour."

The Story of the Craft (The How)

How I Chose to Portray It: I structured the song around a direct contrast between the "rest of the world" (the surface handshake, small talk, screen taps) and the "damned few" (the code, the silent call, the zero-hour). The narrative dismisses the modern, easy forms of communication in favour of primal, purpose-driven action.

The Chosen Focus: I focused on specific imagery that defines high-stakes loyalty:

Dismissing the Shallow (Verse 1 & 2): I established the "enemy" of deep connection through physical actions: the "surface-level handshake" and the "nod on the street." I contrasted the superficiality of "They try to send messages, they tap on the screen" with the true friend who "ignores the message" and reads the "white space."

The Code of Action (Chorus): The Chorus is the anthem of the song. The commitment is defined by action ("show up in the zero-hour") and history ("the history we share"). It explicitly rejects the need for emotional maintenance ("small talk"), asserting that the bond is built to "outlast" the fleeting nature of social life.

The Foundation of Silence (Bridge): The Bridge elevates the bond to a spiritual level, defining it as an unspoken, immutable pact—"No contract was signed, no promise was sworn."

This mutual understanding is a "wavelength of silence," confirming that true connection exists entirely outside the rules of common social interaction.

The Lifeline (The Listen):
https://on.soundcloud.com/41wv61ELiClqJYbu4D

The Lyric

[Verse 1]

The surface-level handshake and the nod on the street

That's how the rest of the world and my shadow will meet.

They know the old version, the story I spun,

The face I put on just to get the job done.

But you saw the darkness, the things that were broke,

Every word that was whispered and every joke.

We don't talk for months, there's no reason to fret,

But the code that was written, we never forget.

[Chorus]

The surface-level handshake is forgotten too fast,

But the code that we live by is built to outlast.

You don't need the small talk, you just hear the silent call,

And you show up in the zero-hour when I'm set to fall.

So lift up your glass to the history we share:

To us and those like us, the damned few who care.

[Verse 2]

They try to send messages, they tap on the screen,

Ask if everything's good, if the landscape is clean.

But you ignore the message, you read the white space,

You move with a purpose to the necessary place.

No questions are wasted, no favours are weighed,

It's the promise we kept, in the fire we made.

You cut through the static, you silence the noise,

You recognise the signal in my shaken voice

[Chorus]

The surface-level handshake is forgotten too fast,

But the code that we live by is built to outlast.

You don't need the small talk, you just hear the silent call,

And you show up in the zero-hour when I'm set to fall.

So lift up your glass to the history we share:

To us and those like us, the damned few who care.

[Bridge]

The years come and go like the tide on the shore,

But the foundation we set can't be shaken anymore.

No contract was signed, no promise was sworn,

Just the mutual understanding the moment we're torn.

It's a wavelength of silence, a frequency clear,

They don't need a map when I signal I'm here.

[Chorus]

The surface-level handshake is forgotten too fast,

But the code that we live by is built to outlast.

You don't need the small talk, you just hear the silent call,

And you show up in the zero-hour when I'm set to fall.

So lift up your glass to the history we share:

To us and those like us, the damned few who care.

[Outro]

Who are our friends?

The damned few who care...

(Fade)

17. I Simply Love You

The Story of the Soul (The Why)

Inspiration: The realisation that after writing many "thoughtful" and complex lyrics, a moment of profound simplicity struck me. My partner popped into my head, and the only, most essential thing I could think of was how much I love her. "Nothing more needs saying."

What I Was Trying to Portray: I intended to communicate the power and purity of love when all complexity and overthinking are removed. The song is a celebration of the truth that love itself is the answer and the only necessary component. By pairing this simple truth with the Reggae rhythm, I aimed to give the emotion a feeling of effortless, universal, and continuous flow.

The Intentional Feeling: I aimed for a feeling of pure, unadulterated joy, rhythm, and peace. The song is designed to feel like a warm, sunny embrace where the emotion is so strong, the only possible lyric is a simple affirmation: "I simply love you."

The Principle of Respectful Space

My Core Intent: This lyric is a joyous, public expression of my devotion. The lack of complexity is a sign of complete certainty and peace within the relationship. By focusing solely on the joy she brings me and the desire to be with her, I affirm the strength of our bond. This song requires no self-defence, no explanation, and no demand; it simply is, fully respecting the self-sustaining nature of our shared love.

The Story of the Craft (The How)

How I Chose to Portray It: I deliberately kept the language accessible and repetitive, mirroring the universal and rhythmic nature of the Reggae genre to ensure the core message—"I simply love you, what more can I say?"—is the absolute takeaway. The verses use simple, sensory imagery of nature and music to amplify the feeling of release and ease.

The Chosen Focus: I focused on sensory and natural metaphors to emphasise the universality of the love:

The Rhythm of Love (Verse 1 & Outro): I integrated the musical genre directly into the emotion: the "reggae rhythm" and "sweet flow" are not just music, but the "path" and the "key to stay." This choice frames the love as natural, easy, and cyclical, like music.

Natural Universals (Verse 1 & 2): I used images of the "ocean breeze," "morning light," "sandy shore," and "stars in the night sky" to assert that this love is not fleeting, but a powerful, natural law—a "universal truth, from sea to bay."

The Essential Truth (Chorus): The Chorus strips away all secondary ideas, boiling the love down to the core declaration. The rhetorical question, "what more can I say?", acts as a final, powerful mic drop, confirming that all further words are unnecessary ornamentation.

The Lifeline (The Listen):
https://on.soundcloud.com/YFTyVBYM4T9eFbpA0m

The Lyric

[Verse 1]

Under the sun, with the ocean breeze,

I feel your love, it's like a sweet release.

In this reggae rhythm, my heart starts to sway,

I simply love you, what more can I say?

You brighten my days, like the morning light,

With every little smile, you set my soul alight.

Your laughter's like music, plays on repeat,

In this dance of life, you make my heart beat.

[Chorus]

I simply love you, baby, can't you see?

Every moment with you is where I wanna be.

It's a universal truth, from sea to bay,

I simply love you, what more can I say?

[Verse 2]

From the moment I met you, I knew it was fate,

With every passing hour, it's you I appreciate.

Walking hand in hand, on this sandy shore,

You're my soulmate forever, I couldn't ask for more.

The stars in the night sky, they shine for us too,

Just like the love we share, forever true.

Through highs and lows, we'll find our way,

In this reggae groove, come what may.

[Chorus]

I simply love you, baby, can't you see?

Every moment with you is where I wanna be.

It's a universal truth, from sea to bay,

I simply love you, what more can I say?

[Bridge]

Through the storms and the rain, we'll stand side by side,

With faith in our hearts, together we'll glide.

Life may throw challenges, we'll rise above,

With a bond so strong, we'll conquer with love.

So let's dance to this rhythm, feel the sweet flow,

With every beat of my heart, I want you to know.

[Verse 3]

As the sun sets down, painting skies in gold,

I'll whisper sweet nothings, in stories untold.

With you in my arms, I'll never feel stray,

I simply love you, what more can I say?

You're the dream that I cherish, my joys and my fears,

With you, I am whole, thank you for the years.

Together forever, that's the path we'll weave,

We'll create our own magic, just believe.

[Chorus]

I simply love you, baby, can't you see?

Every moment with you is where I wanna be.

It's a universal truth, from sea to bay,

I simply love you, what more can I say?

[Outro]

So here's my heart, take it, it's true,

Wrapped in this rhythm, forever with you.

Through every sunrise, I'll find a way,

To simply love you, what more can I say?

Let the reggae play on, let the good vibes sway,

I simply love you, and that's the key to stay.

Part III: The Transcendence and The Human Power (Songs 18-22)

The final resolution, where growth is cemented, and the narrator embraces a resilient, imperfect identity.

18. Every Day is a Good Day

The Story of the Soul (The Why)

Inspiration: The life-altering experience of suffering a cardiac arrest and needing resuscitation in 2016. Before then, I was driven by a job of power and ambition. The experience completely changed my appreciation of life, replacing the hunger for advancement with a desire to "slow things down and smell the coffee." The title comes from the positive reply I always offer when asked how I am.

What I Was Trying to Portray: I intended to communicate the simple, profound truth that existence itself is a miracle and a gift. The song is a declaration that the past ambition and stress are gone, replaced by a life philosophy where every single heartbeat is a blessing. I wanted to show that survival is the ultimate success.

The Intentional Feeling: I aimed to convey a feeling of unshakeable gratitude, peace, and vibrant positivity. The mood is one of celebration, using the Reggae rhythm (like in "I Simply Love You") to give this new outlook a steady, joyful, and universal beat.

The Principle of Respectful Space

My Core Intent: This lyric is a declaration of my internal healing and transformation. By stating "Every day is a good day," I am establishing my own emotional baseline, which is independent of external circumstances or the judgement of others. I respect the space of others by simply offering my conviction as an example, not a demand, finding my own stability by choosing to "live life to the fullest, feeling every little thing."

The Story of the Craft (The How)

How I Chose to Portray It: I structured the song as a contrast between the past darkness and the present light, using repetitive, affirming language in the Chorus to reinforce the central philosophy. The reggae element adds a feeling of communal positivity ("feel the good in the tribe").

The Chosen Focus: I focused on specific imagery of change and gratitude:

The Defining Moment (Verse 1): I immediately established the cause of the transformation: "Resuscitated in 2016, a miracle rather true." This factual detail grounds the entire song's philosophy, explaining that my current happiness is a conscious choice born from a second chance.

The Transformation (Verse 2): I used powerful imagery of renewal, describing the struggle as shadows and the recovery as rising "from the ashes, stand tall like a tree." This emphasises that resilience comes from having overcome the greatest fear.

The Philosophy of the Reply (Verse 1 & Outro): The song builds around the simple reply: "Every day is a good day, come what may." The Outro reinforces this by stating, "So keep on asking, I'll keep on saying," turning the simple greeting into a profound, consistent act of portraying love and positivity.

The Communal Joy (Bridge): The Bridge broadens the philosophy, acknowledging that this new life is shared with a supportive community ("friends all around"), making the personal transformation a source of collective positive energy and defying despair.

The Lifeline (The Listen):
https://on.soundcloud.com/RgmGCqsnz9aeOsFinN

The Lyric

[Verse 1]

When the sun arises, shining so bright,

I step into the morning with everything feeling right.

They ask me how I am, with a smile, I say,

Every day is a good day, come what may.

In the breeze of the moment, I feel alive,

Got a heart full of love, and a soul that thrives.

Resuscitated in 2016, a miracle rather true,

Now I dance to the rhythm, feeling brand new.

[Chorus]

Every day is a good day, that's my vibe,

Living in the moment, feel the good in the tribe.

Every heartbeat's a blessing, counting each and every ray,

With love in my spirit, every day is a good day.

[Verse 2]

I remember the struggle, when shadows came near,

Lost in the dark, facing all of my fears.

But light found a way, shone through the pain,

Now holding on tight, I'll never complain.

So I rise from the ashes, stand tall like a tree,

With roots running deep, I am finally free.

Every laugh, every tear, like a song that I sing,

Living life to the fullest, feeling every little thing.

[Chorus]

Every day is a good day, that's my vibe,

Living in the moment, feel the good in the tribe.

Every heartbeat's a blessing, counting each and every ray,

With love in my spirit, every day is a good day.

[Bridge]

So when the storms roll in, and the clouds cover the skies,

I'll keep my head high, see the sunshine in my eyes.

For every setback's a lesson, turning pain into gain,

Through all of the struggles, I'll never be the same.

I've got friends all around, sharing laughter and cheer,

With every note of reggae, I'm feeling sincere.

We lift each other up, one love in the air,

With a strong positive beat, negating despair.

[Verse 3]

Now I move with the rhythm, let the music unite,

From city to city, oh what a sweet sight.

So when life beckons, and they ask how I feel,

I reply with conviction, oh it's so real.

Through valleys and mountains, with love as my guide,

I'm dancing in harmony, with the world by my side.

So when tomorrow comes and the sun paints the way,

I'll shout it out loud, every day is a good day.

[Outro]

So keep on asking, I'll keep on saying,

With positivity flowing, love is what I'm portraying.

As I walk through the world, feeling joy come what may,

With a smile on my face, I know, every day is a good day.

19. No Regrets

The Story of the Soul (The Why)

Inspiration: The need to directly counter friends who insisted my ex-partner was a "user" and our relationship was a "disaster." I profoundly disagreed. My partner transformed my life, and I experienced my happiest times with her. I feel absolutely no regrets, only a profound gratitude for the golden memories I retain.

What I Was Trying to Portray: I intended to communicate that the ultimate measure of a relationship's success is not its duration or its ending, but the person it creates. The song is a celebration of the self-transformation she sparked—moving me from a life "stuck" and "painted grey" to one of colour, flight, and purpose.

The Intentional Feeling: I aimed to convey a feeling of defiant self-assurance and immense gratitude. The emotion is one of maturity, where I view the breakup not as a "loss" but as the necessary conclusion to a valuable chapter, allowing me to celebrate "the person I am, and the light I haven't lost."

The Principle of Respectful Space

My Core Intent: This lyric is a declaration of my emotional truth, crafted to silence the negative external voices, not to convince my ex-partner of anything. I am defining the experience on my own terms, affirming that I am "just celebrating the person I am" now. By acknowledging that the ending was one of the "unavoidables," I show that I've accepted the lack of control over the outcome and am now responsibly moving forward by choosing to "hold the good, and let the rest fade out."

The Story of the Craft (The How)

How I Chose to Portray It: I used an extended metaphor of motion and stagnant travel (roads, highways, tides, flying) to contrast my life before and after her. The Pre-Chorus is the powerful thesis statement of the entire song, providing a clear, concise rejection of the idea of "lost bets."

The Chosen Focus: I focused on contrasting stagnation with vibrant action:

The Before-State (Verse 1): I established the old life as mechanical and lifeless: the clock going "'round and 'round," the "same four streets," and simply "marking the days off the wall." This sets up the magnitude of her transformative entrance.

The Transformation (Chorus): The Chorus is the core of the argument, using high-impact metaphors: she "ripped the old map right up" and was the "tide that finally swept me away." The ultimate credit is given to her for teaching me "how to fly," cementing her legacy as a catalyst for profound personal growth.

The Acceptance of the End (Pre-Chorus & Bridge): The Pre-Chorus provides the philosophical maturity, accepting that "all good stories have an end." The Bridge references my military-inspired principle from "I am the Road," confirming that I "always knew to control the controllables," and the ending was simply outside of that power, thus preventing regret.

The Colour Motif: I deliberately connected to the colour motif seen elsewhere in the collection by noting that when she walked in, "the colours started to crash," confirming that she brought vibrancy and art back into my world.

The Lifeline (The Listen):
https://on.soundcloud.com/DbBHezGRKvSonPs9Fb

The Lyric

[Verse 1]

The clock just went 'round and 'round,

Same four streets, same tired sound.

I was just marking the days off the wall,

Then you walked in and changed it all.

You ripped the old map right up off the dash,

And suddenly, the colours started to crash.

[Pre-Chorus]

The road we started finally had to bend,

And all good stories have an end.

I could be a punter looking at lost bets, a wreck,

But every moment with you was a winner, baby, no regrets.

[Chorus]

My life was stuck, a highway painted grey,

You were the tide that finally swept me away.

You didn't just teach me how to breathe, you taught me how to fly,

And though that chapter closed, I'm grateful for the sky.

No, I don't regret the miles, or the beautiful, wild cost,

I'm just celebrating the person I am, and the light I haven't lost!

[Verse 2]

We traded the chair for the cold night air.

You showed me stars I had never seen,

And meals we burned, fit for a king and queen.

The miles piled up under a half-tank of gas,

You made every road trip feel like a free pass.

The tent is folded up and put away,

I'm still using the map that you gave me that day.

[Pre-Chorus]

The road we started finally had to bend,

And all good stories have an end.

I could be a punter looking at lost bets, a wreck,

But every moment with you was a winner, baby, no regrets.

[Chorus]

My life was stuck, a highway painted grey,

You were the tide that finally swept me away.

You didn't just teach me how to breathe, you taught me how to fly,

And though that chapter closed, I'm grateful for the sky.

No, I don't regret the miles, or the beautiful, wild cost,

I'm just celebrating the person I am, and the light I haven't lost!

[Bridge]

The hardest part is knowing when to let it go,

When the current changes, the rivers no longer flow.

We did our best, couldn't change the things we couldn't do.

I always knew to control the controllables,

And sometimes, the ending is just one of the unavoidables.

So I'll just hold the good, and let the rest fade out.

[Chorus]

My life was stuck, a highway painted grey,

You were the tide that finally swept me away.

You didn't just teach me how to breathe, you taught me how to fly,

And though that chapter closed, I'm grateful for the sky.

No, I don't regret the miles, or the beautiful, wild cost,

I'm just celebrating the person I am, and the light I haven't lost!

[Outro]

I'm just celebrating the person I am, and the light I haven't lost!

20. Tranquillity

The Story of the Soul (The Why)

Inspiration: A reflection on the changing nature of happiness. For me now, happiness is defined not by ambition or external success, but as a state absent of worry and doubt. This was sparked by visualising simple, peaceful scenarios: sitting by water, hearing children's laughter, or falling asleep to rain on the window.

What I Was Trying to Portray: I intended to communicate that tranquillity is an internal state achieved through heightened awareness of the simple, present moment. The song is an argument that peace is found by actively tuning into the senses and allowing the world to exist without resistance or judgement.

The Intentional Feeling: I aimed to convey a feeling of deep, meditative calm and mindful contentment. The core emotion is one of restful security, achieved by embracing the simple reality of the "here and the now."

The Principle of Respectful Space

My Core Intent: This lyric is a blueprint for my own mental peace. By defining happiness as the absence of my own "worry and doubt," I am taking complete responsibility for my emotional state. I respect the space of others by finding my contentment in observing the world (the children playing, the rain tapping) without needing them to fulfil a specific role. My tranquillity is self-sustaining.

The Story of the Craft (The How)

How I Chose to Portray It: I structured the song around a journey through three distinct, sensory-rich settings that define my tranquillity: Nature (riverbank), Community (playground), and

Solitude (nightfall in bed). The Chorus serves as the thesis statement, unifying these experiences into a single mindful state.

The Chosen Focus: I focused on heightening the sensory details of the environment:

Nature as Orchestra (Verse 1): I used auditory and visual details to create an immersive scene of natural peace: "gentle ripples whisper," a "melodious tease," and a "dragonfly skips." This establishes the external world as a source of effortless calm.

Community as Joy (Verse 2): I moved the scene to a public space, focusing on sound and connection without requiring effort. The "children are laughing" and the "smiles all around" affirm that the world's inherent vitality can contribute to my peace without becoming a source of stress.

The Comfort of Solitude (Verse 3): I used the intimate, cosy imagery of the sound of "soft rainfall on the window" whilst being "under my duvet" to show that even the approach of sleep is a form of active, embraced comfort, freeing my troubled mind.

The Mindful Thesis (Chorus): The Chorus explicitly defines the state: "Awareness heightened," and realising that this appreciation of the simple is "where I truly belong," turning simple observation into a philosophical grounding.

The Lifeline (The Listen):

https://on.soundcloud.com/9V34jtbKdIGNSMV2yk

The Lyric

[Verse 1]

By the river's edge, I find my peace,

The gentle ripples whisper, never cease.

Light breeze dances through the tall green trees,

Nature's soft orchestra, a melodious tease.

A dragonfly skips, with wings all aglow,

Floating on air as it dips down low.

Bees are at work, buzzing joyfully near,

In this tranquil moment, my worries disappear.

[Chorus]

Tranquillity wraps me, in the here and the now,

With every breath, I feel the bliss somehow.

Awareness heightened, as the world passes by,

Appreciating the simple, beneath the vast sky.

In the sights and the sounds, I discover my song,

Every little heartbeat, where I truly belong.

[Verse 2]

Strolling through life, my footsteps in tune,

Children are laughing under the sun's warm bloom.

A playground alive, where joy knows no bounds,

Greeting fellow souls, with smiles all around.

With every shared glance, the connection is real,

In this vibrant world, I truly can feel.

The rhythm of life, it carries me along,

With each little moment, I hum my own song.

[Chorus]

Tranquillity wraps me, in the here and the now,

With every breath, I feel the bliss somehow.

Awareness heightened, as the world passes by,

Appreciating the simple, beneath the vast sky.

In the sights and the sounds, I discover my song,

Every little heartbeat, where I truly belong.

[Verse 3]

Nightfall whispers, as I fight back the sleep,

Under my duvet, oh, the comfort so deep.

Looking forward to dreams where I float and I soar,

Soft rainfall on the window, nature's gentle roar.

With each drop that taps, I drift further away,

Into realms of wonder, I'm ready to sway.

In this quiet embrace, worries fade to the breeze,

Embracing the calm, my troubled mind frees.

[Chorus]

Tranquillity wraps me, in the here and the now,

With every breath, I feel the bliss somehow.

Awareness heightened, as the world passes by,

Appreciating the simple, beneath the vast sky.

In the sights and the sounds, I discover my song,

Every little heartbeat, where I truly belong.

21. Freedom to be You

The Story of the Soul (The Why)

Inspiration: My friend separating from a controlling partner and staying with me. When she asked to celebrate the breakup, the lyric was born from my immediate desire to provide a safe space where, free from coercion, she could fully find herself again.

What I Was Trying to Portray: I intended to communicate that true love is the ultimate liberation. I wanted to define my role as a supportive foundation—the "open road"—not a source of control. The song is a promise that I will stand beside her, dedicated to her self-discovery, and that our closeness is an expansion of her freedom, not a limit on it.

The Intentional Feeling: I aimed to convey a feeling of secure, expansive hope and protective commitment. The mood is one of forward motion and gentle encouragement, emphasising that her heart and soul "will expand" in this new, healthy environment.

The Principle of Respectful Space

My Core Intent: This lyric is a declaration of respect for my partner's absolute agency. I explicitly reject the controlling relationship model by stating: "I'm not a port to hold you fast, No chain to weigh you down." I am committed to creating a relationship where she is the "artist," and I am merely a supportive "colour you can use." My ultimate goal is to give her "The freedom to be you," affirming that my role is to facilitate her growth, not dictate it.

The Story of the Craft (The How)

How I Chose to Portray It: I built the song around contrasting metaphors for movement and safety. I framed myself as temporary rest stops ("safe place when you need a rest") and open avenues ("open road"), rather than fixed objects (ports, chains). The use of the Reggae rhythm (noted in the Outro) gives the love a light, flowing, and unburdened feeling.

The Chosen Focus: I focused on imagery that defines a supportive, non-coercive role:

The Road vs. The Destination (Verse 1): I immediately defined my role not as the goal ("Not a destination or an end") but as the "open road"—the means by which she can pursue her own path. I am a "silent promise" to clear the way.

The Whisper and the Flight (Verse 2): I used gentle, expansive imagery: I am a "whisper in the wind," and a force "behind your flight." This shows I will support her without ever being loud or controlling, allowing her spirit to be lifted so she can "fly" independently.

The Artistic Agency (Bridge): The Bridge is the most direct statement of her autonomy. By calling her the "artist" and the "plan," and myself only a "colour," I make it clear that she is in full control of the canvas of her life, and our relationship is simply a beautiful addition to her already established truth.

The Lifeline (The Listen):
https://on.soundcloud.com/VZY8YdnPddOaqB9UKD

The Lyric

[Intro]

Oh, let the rhythms flow, with the breeze so free,

I want to be the guiding light, come and follow me.

[Verse 1]

I want to be the open road you find,

A wide horizon just for you.

Not a destination or an end,

But the freedom to be new.

I'll walk beside you in the quiet,

A silent promise you can trust,

To clear the way so you can rise,

And leave behind what turned to dust.

[Chorus]

Oh, we'll travel far, hand in hand,

Through valleys low and mountains grand.

Your heart, your soul, they will expand,

With love and hope, we'll make our stand.

[Verse 2]

I'm not a port to hold you fast,

No chain to weigh you down.

Just a safe place when you need a rest,

The quietest part of town.

I'll be a whisper in the wind,

A gentle force behind your flight,

To lift your spirit, help you fly,

And fill your world with light.

[Chorus]

Oh, we'll travel far, hand in hand,

Through valleys low and mountains grand.

Your heart, your soul, they will expand,

With love and hope, we'll make our stand.

[Bridge]

You are the artist, you are the plan,

The canvas is your own.

I'm just a colour you can use,

A truth you've always known.

That being close is not a limit,

And building a life together too.

It's just another way to give,

The freedom to be you.

[Verse 3]

Every step we take, we'll carve our path,

Through storms and sunny skies, we'll never look back.

Through the echoes of laughter, through sorrow's song,

We'll face it together, where we belong.

So when the road gets tough, and the night falls deep,

Just remember the promise, the love we keep.

[Chorus]

Oh, we'll travel far, hand in hand,

Through valleys low and mountains grand.

Your heart, your soul, they will expand,

With love and hope, we'll make our stand.

[Outro]

And I'll be there, through thick and thin,

In the dance of life, together we spin.

With every sunrise, a brand new chance,

To embrace this journey, a sweet romance.

So take my hand, let's walk anew,

In this reggae rhythm, it's just me and you.

Yeah, we'll find our peace, we'll chase the sky,

With open hearts, together we'll fly.

22. I Am Only Human

The Story of the Soul (The Why)

Inspiration: A moment of necessary catharsis after realising I had spent too much time dwelling on past mistakes and regrets in earlier lyrics. I was inspired to write a lyric that shouts out the truth: I try to be good, but I am a flawed human being. The core philosophy is that progress is better than perfection, and the goal is to do my best and get on with enjoying life.

What I Was Trying to Portray: I intended to communicate the liberation that comes from rejecting the impossible standard of perfection. The song defines my new power as residing in my imperfections and my capacity to learn. I wanted to replace the crushing weight of the "invisible checklist" with the joyful acceptance of the "messy, winding road."

The Intentional Feeling: I aimed to convey a feeling of triumphant self-acceptance, defiance, and relief. The emotion moves from the exhausted striving of the past to the energised, celebratory declaration that "I am only human, and that is my power."

The Principle of Respectful Space

My Core Intent: This lyric is a final, definitive boundary with my own inner critic. By proclaiming that I reserve the right to "trip and to rise," I am granting myself the freedom to be imperfect. This internal forgiveness is crucial, as it stops me from projecting perfectionist demands onto others and frees me from needing their external validation. My acceptance of my own flaws allows me to offer genuine, non-judgemental space to the world.

The Story of the Craft (The How)

How I Chose to Portray It: I structured the song around a dramatic comparison between the stagnant "perfect line" of the past and the dynamic, "messy, winding road" of the present. I used bold, declarative language in the Chorus to make the transition from anxiety to acceptance feel like a powerful, immediate break.

The Chosen Focus: I focused on contrasting imagery of control versus liberation:

The Prison of Perfection (Verse 1): I used corporate and mechanical metaphors to define the old life: a "red, constant light," an "invisible checklist," and being "worn out from the performance." This establishes the high-cost, unsustainable nature of that ambition.

The Moment of Clarity (Pre-Chorus): This section is the philosophical pivot. I state that the moment I "dropped the pen and let the whole system fall," I recognised that the beauty of the story is the "struggle on the way," validating my entire messy journey.

The Power of Flaw (Chorus): The Chorus redefines the word "human" as a source of strength, not weakness. I rejected the idea of being a "machine built for the zero hour" (a nod back to earlier lyrics). The scars are transformed into "proof" of being alive and learning, which is the ultimate form of success.

The New Philosophy (Bridge): I shifted the focus from achievement to being. The future is described not as a plan but as a "work that's never fully planned"—a constant, messy motion. The final message is one of internal celebration: "You are the celebration and the stage!"

The Lifeline (The Listen):

https://on.soundcloud.com/6XGvJIQ2KOjCBf3c7x

The Lyric

[Verse 1]

I used to live by the flicker of a red, constant light,

Believed that perfection was the only way to get things right.

I kept an invisible checklist and I signed off every night,

Trying to keep the margin wide, trying to win the inner fight.

I measured every minute, every move, every single glance,

Worn out from the performance, still waiting for a decent chance.

I couldn't breathe, I couldn't move, just building walls I had to climb, Spent a lifetime running out of time.

[Pre-Chorus]

But one morning, I woke up, and the light changed its hue.

I saw the truth reflected in everything I never got through.

The moment I finally dropped the pen and let the whole system fall,

I realised the greatest flaw was believing I wasn't enough at all.

That perfect line I chased was just a flat, lifeless display,

And the beauty of the story is the struggle on the way!

[Chorus]

I am only human, and that is my power,

I'm not a machine built for the zero hour!

I reserve the right to trip and to rise,

With honest sweat in my eyes.

This messy, winding road? It's the map I drew,

I'm not waiting for perfect, some progress will do!

Yeah, I've got my scars, but they're just the proof,

That I'm alive, I'm learning, and I'm breaking the roof!

[Verse 2]

They told me to sand down the edges, keep the story neat and
straight, Said the cracks in the foundation would be sealed up by
the weight.
But I learned that the wrong turns were the scenic roads I had to
roam, And the places I felt weakest are the places I now call home.
My rhythm's off the beat, my timing is my own unique pace, I
don't need a gold trophy just to finish the race. I used to dread the
falling, now I watch how high I bounce— 'Cause the only opinion
that matters is the one that truly counts.

[Instrumental Break]

[Bridge]

Don't let the shadows of yesterday tell you where you have to stand,

We are all just living drafts, a work that's never fully planned.

And the beauty of the blueprint isn't what it will become,

It's the constant, messy motion of the heart beating like a drum.

There's no finish line for me now, there's just turning of the page— You are the celebration and the stage!

[Chorus]

I am only human, and that is my power,

I'm not a machine built for the zero hour!

I reserve the right to trip and to rise,

With honest sweat in my eyes.

This messy, winding road? It's the map I drew,

I'm not waiting for perfect, some progress will do!

Yeah, I've got my scars, but they're just the proof,

That I'm alive, I'm learning, and I'm breaking the roof!

[Outro]

I am only human... and that is my power!

23. Just Wanted You to Know

The Story of the Soul (The Why)

Inspiration: The memory of the first time I went camping with my partner. The woman who was typically uncomfortable with emotional closeness curled into me with a slight smile and hugged me as she was falling asleep. This moment of pure, unconscious vulnerability brought me a feeling of unadulterated joy. The lyric is an imagined whispered conversation with her about that night.

What I Was Trying to Portray: I intended to communicate that the single, unguarded moment of her emotional surrender was the pinnacle of our relationship. The song is an argument that this memory is a "priceless treasure" that outweighs all subsequent pain or loss. I wanted the listener to understand the depth of that emotional connection through her unplanned, instinctive gesture.

The Intentional Feeling: I aimed to convey a feeling of overwhelming, enduring joy and intimacy. The emotion is so powerful that it still makes my eyes "fill up"—not with sadness, but with a "brimming cup" of gratitude and awe for the genuine "miracle" I witnessed.

The Principle of Respectful Space

My Core Intent: This lyric is the ultimate act of respectful, non-demanding love. The entire conversation is imagined and whispered, emphasising that the moment itself was sacred and private. I will not "complain" about her absence, because I possess a memory of her choosing closeness that no external change can diminish. The memory is a self-sustaining source of happiness that requires no present action from her.

The Story of the Craft (The How)

How I Chose to Portray It: I structured the song around intimate, physical micro-details (the finger lifting the hair, the palm touching the face) to make the scene feel as immediate and real as possible. The rhythm of the lyric feels slow and careful, mirroring the gentle, cautious movements I made that night.

The Chosen Focus: I focused on contrasting her normal guardedness with her sleeping vulnerability:

The Intimate Observation (Verse 1): I established the careful, non-intrusive nature of the moment. I was checking her breathing and moving her hair "just so you wouldn't know." This highlights the tenderness and secrecy of the observation.

The Artistic Metaphor (Pre-Chorus & Verse 2): I wanted to connect this moment back to my partner's love of art (as noted in "The Unfinished Embrace") by stating: "You were a canvas that moved and that breathed, The purest work of art I ever believed." This confirms that her unconscious presence was the most beautiful, truthful expression of herself.

The Eternal Value (Chorus & Bridge): The Chorus delivers the core message: the memory is a treasure "gold could never gain." The Bridge reinforces this by stating I wouldn't trade that moment for "anything you could buy," affirming that the value of the experience is infinite and preserved, perfectly "tucked right here."

The Final Whisper (Outro): The spoken/whispered Outro perfectly concludes the entire collection on a note of gentle, eternal connection, bringing the imagined conversation to a quiet close.

The Lifeline (The Listen):

https://on.soundcloud.com/7a4EcojvRe3PxBbVfI

The Lyric

[Verse 1]

Remember that time, just watching you sleep?

I'd check your breathing, a secret I'd keep.

I'd use my finger, so careful and slow,

To lift a strand of hair, just so you wouldn't know.

And my palm would follow, a touch on your face,

Just feeling the peace of that moment and place.

[Pre-Chorus]

You'd give me that smile—that little, tired thing—

And you made me believe in everything.

[Chorus]

And I'm just telling you, my eyes still fill up.

It's not sadness, it's a brimming cup

Of something I saw, a miracle I knew.

And that memory's priceless, baby, all because of you.

Yeah, I miss you, but I won't complain,

I've got the kind of treasure gold could never gain.

[Verse 2]

It wasn't just how you looked in the light,

It was watching your thoughts as they moved through the night.

The way your eyes would shift, that sideways, quick glance,

You'd mouth a silent word, giving thought a chance.

That little movement, your expression would change,

A whole living story you never had to arrange.

[Pre-Chorus]

You were a canvas that moved and that breathed,

The purest work of art I ever believed.

[Chorus]

And I'm just telling you, my eyes still fill up.

It's not sadness, it's a brimming cup

Of something I saw, a miracle I knew.

And that memory's priceless, baby, all because of you.

Yeah, I miss you, but I won't complain,

I've got the kind of treasure gold could never gain.

[Bridge]

I wouldn't trade that moment for anything you could buy.

It's tucked right here, something I hold high.

A perfect picture, breathing in my mind,

The best that I had, the best I could find.

[Outro - Spoken/Whispered]

Just wanted you to know...

I still see that smile.

Yeah.

I still see it.

Conclusion: The Power of the Authentic Scars

Here we stand at the end of this shared journey—a journey not through fictional concepts, but through the unflinching honesty of a life transformed. This body of work, born from moments of deep introspection, heartbreak, and overwhelming gratitude, was ultimately crafted to achieve a single, liberating goal: to prove that the most beautiful stories are the ones we tell without a filter.

If there is one insight from this process that can inspire your own creative or personal path, it is this: Your scars are your greatest source of power.

This entire collection, which you now hold, is a testimony to the radical vulnerability of writing directly from the heart. Every line, every metaphor, and every emotional shift you have encountered is a moment of emotional nakedness. The only muse, the only driver of this process, was the truth of what moved me—whether it was the awe of a simple, intimate moment or the profound pain of a lesson learned. This is not just a songbook; it is a declaration that inspiration is found only when you refuse to armour yourself, using the lyric as a tool to capture feeling with uncompromising authenticity.

The Blueprint for Finding Your Voice

The lyrics contained here trace a specific, hard-won trajectory. To find your own voice, whether in art or in life, consider the blueprint revealed in this collection:

1. Define Your Own Success, Not Perfection

We began stuck in the old rhythm—the life of the "highway painted grey," marked by an endless, internal checklist. The breakthrough came not through achieving a flawless result, but through the radical declaration: "I am only human, and that is my power." To be authentic is to stop waiting for the zero hour. It is to choose progress over perfection and to embrace the messy, winding road you drew yourself.

2. Trade Ambition for Gratitude

The moment that shattered the old life (the cardiac event) became the ultimate source of new, vibrant perspective. This taught me that the greatest success is not external advancement, but the ability to stop and "smell the coffee." In your own life, find your second chance, however small, and use it to build a philosophy where "Every Day is a Good Day"—not because life is easy, but because existence itself is a miracle.

3. Choose Deep Loyalty Over Shallow Connection

Reject the noise of the "surface-level handshake." True companionship—the kind that can hold you in the zero-hour—is rare. Honour the silent, powerful code of "Those Like Us, the damned few who care." I hope that my work shows that a relationship's value is not measured by its duration, but by its unspoken, absolute loyalty and its commitment to granting "The Freedom to be You."

4. The Unconscious Moment is the Priceless Treasure

The truest expressions of love were found not in grand declarations, but in unconscious, unplotted acts—the way a partner curled into you whilst sleeping, or the little smile that caught your eye. These are the "pieces of gold" that hold infinite value. In your own writing and life, train yourself to see the miracle in the simple, instinctive gestures; they are the most honest truths we possess.

Go Be Led by Your Own Light

This is the final encouragement: You have the story, you have the emotional depth, and you have the strength—the fire—to forge your path.

Be unapologetic about your past; declare "No Regrets." Let the pain of the lost bets transform you into someone who is only left with a profound gratitude for the light they haven't lost.

To the reader, and to the writer: May you always find the quiet confidence to declare the truth of your scars, and may your voice be your ultimate, liberating drumbeat.

Go n'éirí an bothar leat!